The Ultimate
BIRDHOUSE BOOK

The Ultimate
BIRDHOUSE BOOK

40 FUNCTIONAL,
FANTASTIC &
FANCIFUL HOMES
TO MAKE FOR OUR
FEATHERED FRIENDS

DEBORAH MORGENTHAL

A Sterling/Lark Book
Sterling Publishing Co., Inc.   New York

DEDICATION

To my husband, Frank Matthews, friend to birds and other wildlife:
May you continue to walk softly in the woods and in my life.

Art Director: Kathleen Holmes
Production: Kathleen Holmes
Production Assistance and Computer Illustrations: Bobby Gold
Photography: Evan Bracken
Illustrations: Olivier Rollin

Library of Congress Cataloging-in-Publication Data
Morgenthal, Deborah, 1950-
     The ultimate birdhouse book : 40 functional, fantastic & fanciful
homes to make for our feathered friends / Deborah Morgenthal.
          p.   cm.
     "A Sterling/Lark book."
     Includes index.
     ISBN 0-8069-0451-8
     1. Birdhouses--Design and construction.
     QL676.5.M66   1997
     690'.8927--dc21
                                                          97-13333
                                                          CIP

10 9 8 7 6 5 4 3 2 1

A Sterling/Lark Book

Published by Sterling Publishing Company, Inc.
387 Park Avenue South, New York, NY 10016

© 1997, Lark Books

Distributed in Canada by Sterling Publishing,
     c/o Canadian Manda Group, One Atlantic Avenue,
     Suite 105, Tornonto, Ontario, Canada M6K 3E7

Distributed in Great Britian and Europe by Cassell PLC,
     Wellington House, 125 Strand, London, England WC2R 0BB

Distributed in Australia by Capricorn Link (Australia) Pty Ltd.,
     P.O. Box 6651, Baulkham Hills Business Centre, NSW 2153, Australia

Additional photo credits

Richard Babb: field, page 13; pond, page 63;
Bill Duyck: Carolina wren, page 13, bluebird,
page 63; Bill Lea: chickadee, pages 6 and 101,
cardinal, page 13, boat-tailed grackle and
tufted titmouse, page 47, flicker, page 63,
warbler, page 101; Darlene Polachic, page 98.

Printed in Hong Kong by Oceanic Graphic Printing Productions Ltd.

ISBN 0-8069-0451-8

CONTENTS

Miniature gourd birdhouses, designed by Ginger Summit

INTRODUCTION

Every spring for several years, a Carolina wren has built a nest in the mosaic birdhouse hanging on our back porch, a gift from friend Terry Taylor (his work appears on pages 78 and 95). I think it is the same wren, but I am not enough of an ornithologist to be positive. I love the sight and sound of this social, noisy bird efficiently building one of several nests, in the hope that the female will deem one of them worthy. The first year that she chose the one in our hanging birdhouse, I peeked in to catch a glimpse of the eggs and was aggressively chased away by mommy wren. I have respected her space ever since.

My husband, Frank, once a small manufacturer of cedar birdhouses and feeders, now a nurse, and always an artist and friend to wildlife, has stocked our yard with the last of his product line. A honeysuckle bush, located next to one of his large feeders, is a popular meeting place for a dozen or more cardinals. Having these gorgeous, shy birds as neighbors makes us feel blessed. In fact, along with the distant sound of traffic, an occasional freight train, and the chatter of squirrels, our family is serenaded with the music of a remarkable chorus of mourning doves, wrens, blue jays, tufted titmice, robins, nuthatches, crows, flickers, song sparrows, towhees, and starlings. My five-year-old daughter, Corrina, delights in finding our pecan tree filled at sunset with talkative starlings, who, she is sure, are having a tea party. She listens to them for a moment, claps her hands, and (what power!) startles into flight more starlings than she can count.

I am sure many of you can relate to these anecdotes. What gives them, perhaps, extra meaning is that we live, not in a remote wooded location, but in the suburbs of a small city. Through a combination of planning and luck, we have created an appealing habitat for a remarkable variety of birds. In addition to the selfish pleasure of seeing so many different birds right out the kitchen window, we are also

helping to ensure their survival. Each year, wildlife organizations acquire and manage millions of acres of wetland habitat—swamps, ponds, lakes, and marshes—that provide nesting habitats for songbirds and shorebirds, ducks and geese, hawks and owls. But as more and more natural resources give way to housing developments and office parks, it has become increasingly important that people living in the suburbs, the city, and the country offer birds a hospitable environment where they can thrive. As "Attracting Birds" describes (see page 31), it is neither difficult nor expensive to provide our feathered friends with food, water, and a place to rest and nest, no matter where you live.

The 40 birdhouses in this book were designed by people who usually make other kinds of objects, but who agreed to make a birdhouse because they like birds. In fact, only one designer, Robin Clark, builds birdhouses for a living, and he and one of his star employees, Cathy Smith, ascended to new heights with their designs, as the Adobe Hideaway demonstrates (page 20).

The nest boxes these 20 designers created exhibit a wonderful range of style and attitude. From the classical Bluebird Cathedral by George Harrison (page 71), to the outrageous Emerald City by Pat Schieble (page 76), to the remarkable replica of an Appalachian Farm Smokehouse by Don Stevenson (page 24), there is a nest box here certain to please the tastes of builder and bird alike. There are even a handful of projects that started as birdhouses but became something else altogether, such as the Egyptian Birdhouse CD Holder by Diane Weaver (page 102).

Some of the projects were designed for a specific type of bird. If you like the Carolina Wren House (page 48) but want to attract a flicker, simply refer to the Nest

Dimensions chart on page 125, and modify the instructions as necessary. A good percentage of the projects will stand up to the vagaries of weather; others will do better on a sheltered porch. A few are so exquisitely decorated that you may want to display them in the living room, and not share them with the birds at all. The choice is yours.

Most of the birdhouses in this book require working with wood and using power tools. If you are new to wood-working, you may want to refer to a basic woodworking text before you tackle some of the projects. Some woodworkers may decide to follow the instructions to the last pilot hole; others may prefer to use the instructions as a jumping-off point, modifying them as they see fit. This is also up to you.

It was great fun throwing out seeds of ideas to designers and watching what flew in. We hope the projects in this book feed your creativity so that you can offer a bird a really great place to nest and raise a family. Make one or two or ten. Mount them in the right place at the right time. Then, go away, please, and let nature take its course.

GALLERY OF BIRDHOUSES

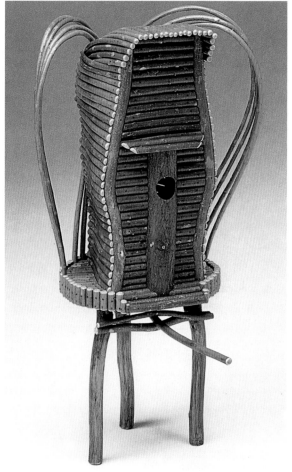

All designs by Clifton Monteith, Lake Ann, MI
Top left: *Willow and Aspen Birdhouse*
Top right: *Willow and Cedar Birdhouse*
Bottom: *Willow, Aspen, and Cedar Birdhouse*

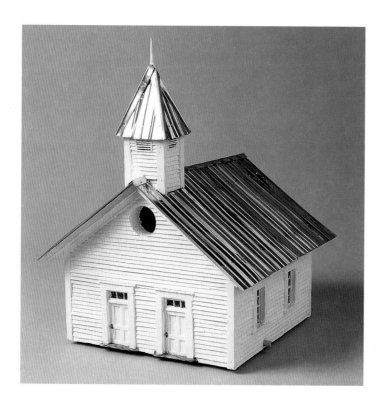

All designs by Don Stevenson, Morganton, NC
Top left: *Mariahs Chapel United Methodist Church*
Top right: *Rutherford County Smokehouse*
Bottom left and right: *Mail Pouch Billboard
Barn and Hayloft* (front and back)
(wood, aluminum sheeting, paint)

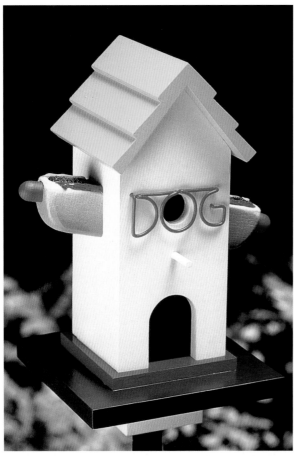

Top left: Randy Sewell,
Atlanta, GA, *Dog House*
(wood, fiberglass, wire)

Top right: Randy Sewell
Ball Park (wood, wire)

Bottom left: Marilyn Rehm,
Big Prairie, OH,
Carved Gourd Birdhouse

Bottom right: Marilyn Rehm
Carved Gourd Birdhouse

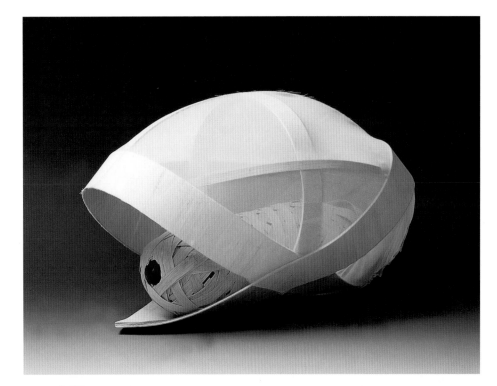

Right: Thomas Stender,
Chicago, IL, *Ariel*
(maple strips, reed, silk)

Bottom left: John Payne,
Swannanoa, NC, *Pyramid Birdhouse*
(metal)

Bottom right: Jonathan Adler
New York, NY, *Ceramic Birdhouses*

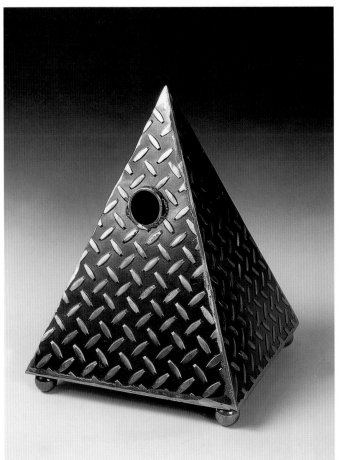

11

Top left: Sheila Sheppard, Jonesborough, TN
La Juala (polymer clay)

Top right: Harold Hall, Kent, OH
Storybook Birdhouse (gourd)

Bottom left and right: Lady Slipper Designs, Bemidji, MN
Architectural Birdhouses (wood)

Many birds including the Carolina wren (top) and the cardinal (bottom) are attracted to untamed backyards, so leave a corner of your yard wild, if possible.

Two-Family Patterned Birdhouse

DESIGN: **Diane Weaver**

The pairing of subtle patterns with subdued colors makes this double-decker doubly beautiful.

Materials and Supplies

Two-story wooden birdhouse*
2 decorative wooden dowels, 1⅝" long
Basswood, ½" x 1" x 3'*
4 wooden honey dippers
Pencil
Straightedge
Wood filler
Sandpaper
Wood glue
Paintbrushes
Acrylic primer
Acrylic paint in dusty khaki, deep khaki,
   and ice blue
½" brads
*available in craft-supply stores

Tools

Drill and drill bits
Jigsaw
Wood clamp
Tack hammer
¼" x 6" wood dowel sharpened to a fine point
   in a pencil sharpener
Paint-combing tool (optional)

Instructions

1. Drill a hole ¾" down from both entrance holes, wide enough to fit the decorative dowels. Drill holes in the base of the house to fit the stems of the honey dippers.

2. Measure and cut the basswood for the base skirt, cutting the side strips first so that they are flush with the ends of the base. Then cut the front and back strips so they overlap the ends of the side strips.

3. Trace a pattern of waves on one of the strips, keeping the waves an equal distance from both ends. Clamp the wood securely and cut out the waves with the saw. Sand well to remove any rough cuts. Trace the wavy pattern onto the other three strips and cut and sand them in the same way.

4. Glue and tack the strips in place.

5. Glue the honey dippers and perches in position.

6. Fill, sand, and prime the house, dowels, and perches. Let dry.

7. Paint the main body of the house with deep khaki and let dry. Paint the front edge and underside of the roof, the trim boards that separate the floors, the inside edges of the entrance holes, the base, the perches, and the feet blue. Let dry.

8. With a straightedge and pencil, draw lines to divide sections of the house geometrically. Start with the roof: Measure its length and width and divide the dimensions into squares of equal size. Cover one square at a time with a coat of dusty khaki and then draw lines through the wet paint with the point of the sharpened dowel or the combing tool. Vary the patterns from square to square with crosshatched, wavy, horizontal, vertical, diagonal, spiral, and curvy lines. On the lower level sides, plan your geometric design around the square in which you will paint the bird patterns.

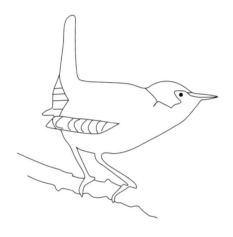

Frank Lloyd Wright Wren House

DESIGNER: **George Harrison**

Mr. Wright, one of America's greatest and most well known architects, would probably be pleased to lend his name to this handsome cypress birdhouse, designed with the dramatic lines and overhangs that often distinguished his work.

CUT LIST

1" cypress

> A: 10½" x 7¾" (1)
>
> B: 1" x 9¾" (1)
>
> C: 8" x 8" (1)
>
> D: 1" x 9½"
>
> E: 6½" x 8" (1)
>
> F: 2" x 6½" (1)
>
> G: 4" x 6½" (1)
>
> H: 2" X 7½" (1)
>
> I: 6¼" x 5" (1)
>
> J: 9½" x 8" (1)

MATERIALS AND SUPPLIES

> Carpenter's glue
>
> 2" brads
>
> 1½" decking screws
>
> Wood putty
>
> Sandpaper

TOOLS

> Table saw
>
> Drill with ¼" bit
>
> Jigsaw
>
> Hammer
>
> Screwdriver

INSTRUCTIONS

1. Measure, mark, and cut four rectangular slots along one 8" side of A; the first groove is 1" in from the end, and the grooves are about ¾" apart.

2. Cut four grooves the same way in C; the first groove is 1" in from the end, and the grooves are about 1¼" apart.

3. Glue B to A, and D to C.

4. Cut a 25-degree angle on one of the 6½" sides of both E and G.

5. Drill a 1¼" entrance hole in J, 5" up from the bottom and 3½" in from the left.

6. Attach A to E and G, then attach E and G to C.

7. Cut a 25-degree angle on one 2" side of H. Glue H to G, with the angled edge flush with the roof.

8. Cut a 45-degree angle on one 6½" side of F. Glue F to E, with the angled edge facing forward.

9. Attach I to E and G with screws. (You can unscrew the back when you need to clean the box.)

10. Fill in the nail and screw holes with wood putty. When dry, sand the entire birdhouse.

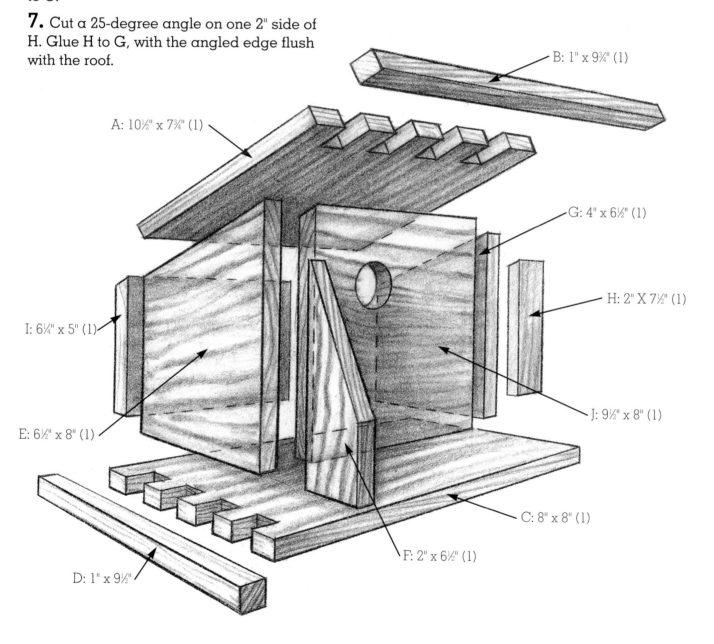

A: 10½" x 7¾" (1)

B: 1" x 9¾" (1)

G: 4" x 6½" (1)

H: 2" X 7½" (1)

I: 6¼" x 5" (1)

J: 9½" x 8" (1)

E: 6½" x 8" (1)

C: 8" x 8" (1)

D: 1" x 9½"

F: 2" x 6½" (1)

ADOBE HIDEAWAY

DESIGNERS: **ROBIN CLARK AND CATHY SMITH**

Complete with miniature cacti and a tiny dream catcher, this house is perfect for birds (and humans) with a craving for desert decor.

CUT LIST

1" pine

   Sides: 7" x 6½" (2)

   Front/back: 4½" x 6½" (2)

   Top: 4½" x 4½" (1)

   Bottom: 7¼" x 13" (1)

Vigas: ½" x 1" dowel (10)

Materials and Supplies

Medium-grit sandpaper
Finish nails
Wood glue
Acrylic matte varnish, 6 to 7 ounces
Paintbrushes, 1" flat bristle and #4 round
Coarse sand, 12 ounces
Fine, white craft sand, 8 ounces
Fine black and green craft sand,
    4 ounces of each
Applicator bottles for craft sand
Cardboard strip, 1" x 5", folded like an
    accordion lengthwise
Toothpick
Acrylic paint in burnt sienna
Spray acrylic matte finish
Green twigs
Heavy thread

Tools

Table saw
Jigsaw
Drill with ¼" and ½" bits
Hammer

Instructions

Building the house

1. Spaced equally 1" down from the top edge, drill five ½" holes, ¼" deep on all pieces except the bottom.

2. On the front piece, drill a 1½" hole, centered, 5¼" from the bottom.

3. Attach the front and back to the roof using nails, then round the edges with sandpaper.

4. Round the edges of the sides, then nail them to the front, back, and roof, letting the sides extend 1" at each end.

5. Glue in the dowels.

6. Mount the house to the bottom with nails, hammered in from the underside of the house.

Creating the adobe effect

7. Sand the birdhouse to remove any splinters and to give the wood "tooth."

8. Paint one side of the house with varnish; apply a fairly thick coat. Cover the wet varnish with a layer of coarse sand. Let dry and repeat with the next side. Don't worry about perfect coverage on this first layer of sand. Apply two more coats of varnish and coarse sand on all surfaces. *Don't apply any varnish or sand to the base or the vigas.* Be sure to allow each layer to dry thoroughly before the next application.

9. On the last layer of varnish and sand, use the accordion-folded cardboard strip to create a pattern of random cracks in the wet sand by placing the pleats flush with the surface and pushing and wiggling the cardboard against the wet sand. Let dry.

10. Apply a last coat of varnish to one side and then cover the wet surface with a layer of fine, white sand. Do one side at a time and be sure to shake off the excess sand. Allow each side to dry completely before moving on to the next surface. *Again, do not apply sand to the bottom or the vigas.*

11. Draw pots and cactus on the walls as desired. Follow step 10, using the black and green sand, to create the potted cacti. It will take about five varnish and sand layers with the black sand and about three varnish and sand layers with the green sand to achieve the effect you want. While the sand is still a little mushy, use a toothpick to create the details in the cacti.

12. Make a very diluted wash with the burnt sienna paint and use it to streak areas of the house to create a weathered look.

13. Mix a small amount of the burnt sienna with the matte varnish and apply a coat to the base and the vigas.

14. When everything is dry, gently dust off the excess sand, then spray on three to four coats of matte finish, letting each coat dry.

15. Make a miniature dream catcher, using the green twigs and the heavy thread.

FLORAL GOURD BIRDHOUSE

DESIGNER: **GINGER SUMMIT**

This pretty gourd birdhouse is easy to make, and the brightly painted flowers are sure to attract the eyes of birds flying by.

MATERIALS AND TOOLS

Mid-size hardshell gourd, cured

Bleach

Rubber gloves

Large plastic dish pan or tub

Plastic or metal kitchen scrubbing pad

Brush with stiff, natural bristles

Compass with pencil

Sandpaper

Paintbrushes

Leather dyes in red, orange, yellow, and leaf
    green*

Exterior varnish, with u.v. inhibitor, if possible

Leather thong, 12" long

could also use acrylic paints

TOOLS

Dull kitchen knife

Drill with ¼" bit

Keyhole or hobby saw, motorized cutting tool,
    or small hand-held power jigsaw

Wood-burning tool

INSTRUCTIONS

1. Soak the gourd in a tub of water into which you have mixed a small amount of bleach. Cover the gourd with an old towel to weigh it down so that the entire gourd is submerged. Soak the gourd for 30 minutes. Scrub off the mold with a scrubbing pad and brush; scrape of stubborn spots with a dull kitchen knife.

2. Study the gourd to determine where you want the entrance hole. Set the radius of the compass to ¾" and draw a circle 1½" in diameter. Drill a ¼" hole in the center of the circle, and then cut the hole.

3. Shake out the seeds and pulp through the hole, then sand the edge of the hole smooth.

4. Drill five small holes in the bottom of the gourd for drainage. Drill a hole on each side of the neck of the gourd for the leather thong.

5. Using the project photograph or other pictures, sketch leaves and flowers onto the surface of the gourd.

6. Carefully, with light pressure, wood burn along the pencil lines.

7. Color your design with leather dyes or acrylic paints. When dry, apply two coats of varnish, letting each coat dry thoroughly.

8. Thread the leather thong through the holes at the top of the gourd and knot the ends together.

APPALACHIAN FARM SMOKEHOUSE

DESIGNER: DON STEVENSON

This 1890s smokehouse, a familiar part of the landscape in the mountains of Tennessee and North Carolina, is rendered with remarkable detail, (please notice the tiny latch on the door), care that will not go unnoticed by a discerning bluebird.

CUT LIST

¾" fir or exterior plywood
    A: Floor—5" x 5" (1)
    B: Front/back—6½" x 12¼" (2)
    C: Sides—6½" x 9¾" (2)

¼" fir or exterior plywood
    D: Roof—6½" x 9½" (1)
    6¾" x 9½" (1)

¹⁄₁₆" oak
    E: Door—⅜" x 30" (see figure 1)
Paneling for door: ³⁄₃₂" x 2½" x 3½" (1)

¹⁄₁₆" treated yellow pine
    F: Clapboard siding—½" x 45'
    G: Corner trim—¾" x 9½" (8)
    H: Smoke vent trim—¼" x 5" (2)

¾" treated yellow pine
    I: Roof shingles—5½" x 10'*

Hardwood dowels
    ½" dia. x ⅜" long (1)
    ⅛" dia. x 1¼" long (1)

The ¾" stock is re-sawn to ⅜" x 1½" x random lengths to accommodate splitting the 350 shingles, each ¹⁄₁₆" x ⅜" x 1½". See steps 20 and 21.

MATERIALS AND SUPPLIES

Carpenter's glue
3d finish nails
4d finish nails
20-gauge brads, ½" long
Wood stain in light-blond oak
Exterior, flat, latex house paint in black, white,
    orange, yellow, dark blue and red
Paintbrushes, 1" brush; no. 6 round and no. 8
    flat artist brushes; ⅜" stencil brush

TOOLS

Table or radial arm saw
Jigsaw
Scroll saw
Band saw
Drill press
Drill with 1½" and ¼" bits
Hammer
Motorized cutting tool with 18-and 20-gauge
    drill bits
Wood vise
Clamps
¾" wood chisel

INSTRUCTIONS

1. Cut a 45-degree angle on both B pieces, along the 12¼" sides, to form the peak at the top and back of the house.

2. Drill a ¼" access hole for the smoke vent, directly below the peak and 3" in from the sides on both B pieces. Then use the scroll saw to cut the 1" x 1½" rectangle.

3. Cut a 20-degree angle along one 6½" side of both C pieces.

Building the door

4. In one of the B pieces, cut a 1½" x 3" door, centered. *(Do not cut the entrance hole at this time.)*

5. Glue a scrap of ³⁄₃₂" paneling inside the front piece to cover the hole cut for the door. Cut the ¹⁄₁₆" x ⅜" oak to the size you need to make the door (you will need four small pieces, as shown in figure 1, page 26). Glue these pieces to the paneling.

6. Cut the dowels to create the door bolt and slide assembly and glue it in place. When all the glue is dry, stain the entire door.

7. Assemble the front, back, and sides with glue and 4d finishing nails. (The inside dimensions of the birdhouse should be 5' x 5' wide by 12¼" high.)

Siding the house

8. Begin by cutting a 5" piece of ¹⁄₁₆" treated yellow pine to a thickness of ⅛"—this is one of your spacer jacks, a key element to the success of siding the birdhouse. This tiny piece of yellow pine will elevate the drip edge (bottom) of the first clapboard you glue on. As you install the second piece of clapboard, the thickness of the first piece will elevate the drip edge of the second piece, and so on, up the side of the structure. Glue the spacer jack in place along the bottom of one side of the house and let dry.

9. Cut the clapboard material into 100 pieces, each 5" long.

10. Glue the first clapboard on top of the spacer jack so it is completely hidden by the clapboard. Continue to add siding all the way up the side. Repeat this process on the other side.

11. Continue to install the clapboard on the front and back of the house, cutting to fit around the door. Trim as necessary to fit the angles as you reach the top of the front and back. Allow the glue to dry for 24 hours.

12. Cut the ¹⁄₁₆" oak for the door trim and the strip above the door (figure 1). Glue and nail in place.

13. Mark the position of the 1½" entrance hole on the front of the house, centered, 6¾" from the bottom. You may want to secure the birdhouse in a drill press for this step. Carefully hammer a 4d finishing nail in the center of where the entrance hole will be, through the clapboards and into the plywood. Remove the nail. Use this hole to begin drilling the 1½" hole. When the drill cuts through the clapboards, try to keep the box as still as possible to prevent breaking off the thin siding material. Use steady pressure on the drill so you do not break through the inside wall too quickly.

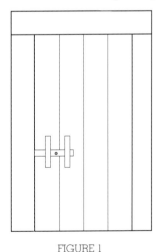

FIGURE 1

14. Glue both D pieces to the house, overlapping the longer one at the ridge, then nail them in place.

15. Using the ¹⁄₁₆" treated yellow pine, trim out the four corners of the building and the gable end (under the eaves) that face along the roof pitch line. This will cover any irregularities showing in the clapboard ends where they meet the roof pitch line. When nailing the corner trim, use 20-gauge brads along and near the inside edge of the trim piece. This will assure the brad finding root in the side wall, not in the actual corner edge. You may want to predrill these nail holes to prevent splitting the trim piece.

16. Fit and position A (the floor) to the bottom of the house. You will need to cut out a notch to allow the floor to clear the entrance door backing. The floor should fit tightly in the bottom, but allow removal without difficulty. If necessary, wedge slivers of scrap wood to make the fit more secure.

Base pin and knob assembly

17. Grip the house upside down in a vise so you have good access to the bottom edge of each side (⅜" from the bottom, centered) where you will drill holes for the dowels. Drill a ⁵⁄₆₄" hole, 1½" deep on both sides (these holes will go through the siding and the sides of the floor).

18. Cut two pieces of ³⁄₁₆" dowel, 2" long. Take the ½" diameter dowel and clamp it in a drill press vice to hold it in the vertical position. Using a ³⁄₁₆" drill bit, drill out the center of this dowel. On a scroll saw, saw this dowel into two lengths, each ½". Fit the ³⁄₁₆" dowel into the ½" knob and glue in place (the dowel should pass all the way into the knob and slightly out the other end, to completely fill the hole.) Make a second pin the same way.

19. Holding the smaller dowel as a handle, sand the knob ends (belt sander or by hand) to round the edges. Insert the assembled pins into the holes in each side of the house. These pins will lock the base of the house to the structure and afford easy access when you need to clean out the birdhouse.

Making roof shingles

20. Set the rip fence on your band saw to 2¾" wide. Run a piece of ¾" x 5½" treated yellow pine through the saw, ripping in equal width strips of ¾" x 2¾" x random widths. Next, move the rip fence and set it ⅜" from the

blade. Now turn the ¾" board up on its ¾" edge and re-saw to a width of ⅜", making certain to always keep the height of the board presented tightly against the fence. Then, saw this long plank into a segment 1½" wide. You should now have a board ⅜" x 1½" x 2¾". Cut several boards in this manner.

21. Clamp a hardwood scrap board, about 5" x 8", to the front edge of your work bench: this will be your chopping block. Place one of the ⅜" x 1½" x 2¾" pine boards you sawed in

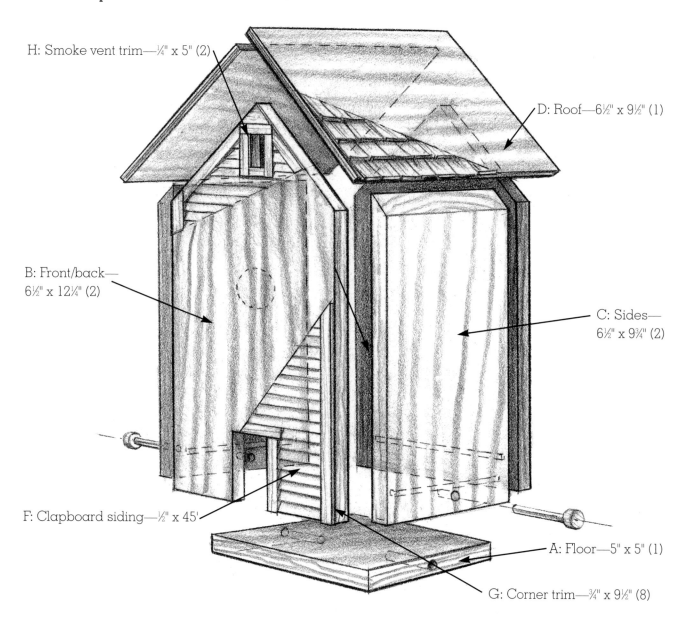

H: Smoke vent trim—¼" x 5" (2)

D: Roof—6½" x 9½" (1)

B: Front/back—6½" x 12¼" (2)

C: Sides—6½" x 9¾" (2)

F: Clapboard siding—½" x 45'

A: Floor—5" x 5" (1)

G: Corner trim—¾" x 9½" (8)

step 20 on the chopping block and hold it as shown in figure 2. The chisel should be set on the board so you can render a shingle $\frac{1}{16}$" thick with one strike. Work very slowly and carefully at first: working with a chisel is the same as working with an ax. (It is wise to be aware of "what you are going to hit when you miss what you are hitting at.") When you chip off the first shingle, check its thickness, and adjust or continue with your next strike. As you feel your way in this process, you will get faster and more deliberate. Be patient and good-humored—you will need both to split 350 shingles!

Adding the shingles

22. The first course of shingles—attached to the bottom, or drip edge, of the roof—is a double course (see photo above right). The second course covers the cracks between the shingles beneath. Along the outside edges of the ascending roof, as each course of shingles is attached, begin or end with a half-width shingle. Start the first course by gluing on the shingles with a $\frac{3}{8}$" overhang. Then, using 20-gauge brads, nail the shingles in place. (It is best to pre-drill four or five nail holes to avoid splitting the shingles.) Once nailed in, you will need to grind the

brads flush with the underside of the roof bed to prevent injury to bird and human alike. You may need to nail and glue the half-width shingles in place, too.

23. Work your way up the roof to the peak. It works best to keep the building at an inclined angle while adding the shingles: if the building is upright, the glue tends to weep between the courses and runs down onto the previous courses installed. The last course of shingles on one side may need to be cut a shorter length to look just right.

24. To complete the traditional look of this building, add a last course of shingles that extends over the longer side of the roof ridge. When these structures were built in the late 1800s, the long side of the roof was the side facing the prevailing weather, and an additional course of shingles was needed to protect the roof crown and its ridge. You will need to glue and nail this last course as you did the first course.

25. Paint the entire structure with flat black exterior latex paint and let dry. Be sure to cover all the irregularities of the shingles. To achieve the weathered look of an old barn, you will want to experiment on scrap wood, using all the colors listed on the materials list, mixing and blending them well.

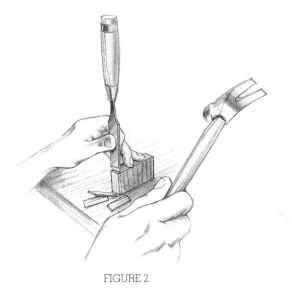

FIGURE 2

LITTLE COUNTRY HOUSE

DESIGNERS: **ROBIN CLARK AND CATHY SMITH**

A simple crackle effect and plenty of wandering flowers give this house its homey look, sure to provide comfort to a swallow or flycatcher in need of a good place to nest.

Cut List

1" maple
> Sides: 6" x 9" (2)
> Floor: 6½" x 9" (1)
> Front/back: 5" x 6" (2)
> Roof: 5¼" x 7½" (2)
> Porch: 3½" x 6½" (1)

⅜" pine
> Posts: ⅜" x 3½" (2)

1¼" pine:
> Chimney: 1¼" x 2 (1)

Materials and Supplies

½" brads
Wood glue
Medium-grit sandpaper
Round sable or synthetic sable paintbrushes,
> #10, #4, #0

Sea sponge
Pencil
Acrylic crackle medium
Acrylic craft paint: cream, charcoal gray, burnt
> sienna, hunter green, bright yellow, bright
> orange, kelly green

Spray acrylic matte finish

Tools

Table saw
Jigsaw
Drill with 1½" bit
Hammer

Instructions

Building the birdhouse

1. Cut the peak on the side pieces by sawing along a line drawn 6" from the bottom to the center on the top.

2. Drill the 1½" entrance hole, centered, 5" from the bottom on the front piece.

3. Attach the sides to the front and back and then attach this assembly to the bottom.

4. Cut a 45-degree angle on one 7½"-edge of each roof piece, and then mount the two roof pieces to the sides with brads.

5. Cut about a 10-degree angle on the porch roof and the top edge of each post. Glue and/or nail the posts to the roof and floor, then glue the roof to the front.

6. Cut a 90-degree angle into the bottom of the chimney, then glue in position on the roof.

Painting the birdhouse

7. Sand the birdhouse to remove splinters and provide "tooth."

8. Apply a base coat of burnt sienna to all surfaces, except the inner edge of the entrance hole. Let dry.

9. Apply the crackle finish on all surfaces, except the porch, chimney, and entrance-hole edge. Your brush strokes will show, but that's okay; just make sure they are all going in the same direction. *Note:* Keep enough paint on your brush for a full stroke. If you try to "fix" a stroke or go over it a second time, the finish will not crack. (If you have never used this medium before, try practicing on a scrap of wood first.) Allow the crackle finish to dry for 24 hours.

10. Paint the posts, front porch, and roof, using the photograph as a guide. Apply two coats of each color for good coverage, allowing each coat to dry thoroughly.

11. Draw the doors, window, shutters, window boxes, and planter boxes onto the birdhouse. Don't draw the details, just the general lines. Base coat these areas in charcoal gray (use the #4 brush). The gray will act as an outline for your brush strokes. Allow to dry completely. Paint in the details. Do not try to be too precise—think impressionist! Use the #0 brush for hard to get places and smaller details (such as the bricks on the chimney, around the door knob, etc.).

12. Wet the sea sponge and dip a small piece of it into a puddle of hunter green—this is your background "shadow" foliage. Blot out the excess paint. Have fun with the foliage—let it pour out of the window boxes and meander around the house. Try not to slide the sponge; you are aiming for a dappled effect. Repeat this procedure with kelly green and yellow. Don't worry about letting the paint dry before you go on to the next color. You want the colors to mix a little. Using dark green, then medium green, then yellow, will create a shadow to sunlight effect. Apply one coat with all the colors and let dry.

13. Paint the flowers with the #0 brush. Alternate yellow flowers/orange centers, with orange flowers/yellow centers. Flower petals are five or six single, radiating brush strokes; the center is a simple dot. Keep your brush heavily loaded with paint so the colors will stay bright.

14. When all the paint is dry, spray the birdhouse with matte finish. Apply three coats, letting each coat dry completely.

ATTRACTING BIRDS

Just as you do not want to live in a house that is inconvenient or inconsistent with your lifestyle, birds are opinionated when shopping for a place to set up housekeeping. In order to attract and keep birds, you will need to provide them with a suitable place to build a nest, as well as water and food.

In choosing a birdhouse, or nesting house, it is essential that you first consider the type of birds you wish to attract. The size of the entrance hole, the depth of the interior, and the height at which the house is mounted should be tailored to the variety you chose. (See the chart on page 125.)

If your goal is to share your yard with a variety of birds, then you should try to offer a varied environment. This means providing several kinds of feeders and a variety of food year round. Bobbe Needham, author of Beastly Abodes, *offers the following suggestions for keeping birds content: "A good basic plan includes a water source, a hanging sunflower seed feeder, a tray feeder (or the ground, if cats aren't a threat) for cracked corn and mixed seed, and a suet feeder (in cold weather only)."*

If you do not have a natural water source close by, you should definitely put a birdbath in your yard. This does not need to be a formal bird bath, but any spot where water can collect. Make sure that a perch is no more than 10 feet away.

You can attract a variety of birds by letting a piece of your yard grow wild. If this is not possible, try creating a brush pile, letting a section of your grass remain unmowed, leaving dead trees or limbs uncut (if they're not dangerous), or planting a patch of wildflowers. Because many birds, such as cardinals, doves, and orioles, do not nest in houses, leave the materials they need to build their nests elsewhere in a basket or a box outside. A good supply of fiber scraps, twigs, wool, feathers, down, bark, moss, paper, and straw will help keep them around. Do make the strips too long—no longer than about 4 inches—since birds can entangle themselves.

Planting shrubs or flowers that produce berries or seeds that birds will eat is also effective. Try honeysuckle, clover, vetch, barberry, juniper, currant, bush cherry, and cotoneaster. Hummingbirds love salvia, petunias, and impatiens. Berry bushes of all kinds are attractive to birds, as are sunflowers, burning bush, and Virginia creeper. Boston ivy is a great choice if you live in the city—birds love its blue fruits. Some small trees that birds enjoy are hawthorn, crab apple, camphor, locust, and redbud. Dogwood is a wonderful source of natural bird food, as it bears autumn fruit. Tall trees, such as pine, spruce, hemlock, birch, elm, maple, and cherry, can also attract birds, since they provide shelter, cones, and seeds.

OCTAGON NEST BOX

DESIGNER: **ROBIN CLARK**

This handsome cedar and redwood house has what it takes to invite an ash-throated flycatcher or a bluebird to spend the spring nesting in your backyard.

Cut List

1" redwood
> A—Base, top/bottom: 10" x 10" (2)

1" cedar
> B—Top/bottom: 4½" x 4½" (2)
> C—Sides: 2¼" x 11" (8)

Materials and Supplies

1¼" decking screws
Sandpaper

Tools

Table or band saw
Jigsaw
Router with ¼" round-over bit (optional)
Drill with 1½" and ⅛" bits
Screwdriver

Instructions

1. Set the saw for a 22½-degree angle and bevel the long edges of every C piece.

2. Drill a ⅛" pilot hole, centered, top and bottom, about ⅜" from the ends of these cedar strips.

3. On one strip, center and drill the 1½" entrance hole, approximately 8" from the bottom, and round-over the edge.

4. Cut the two B pieces into octagons, with side lengths equal to the inside width of the cedar strips. Drill two ⅛" pilot holes in each piece, spaced equally from one another.

5. From one of the A pieces of redwood, cut an 8½" octagon (the sides will be about 3½") for the top, then round the edges with a router or sandpaper. From the other A piece, cut a 7" octagon (the sides will be about 2¾") for the bottom. Round the edges.

6. Center the smaller A piece on top of one of the B pieces, and attach them with screws. Do the same with the other A piece and B piece.

7. Place the larger A/B combination on your work surface, with the small octagon facing up. Carefully line up one cedar strip with a side of the B piece, and attach it with screws.

Mount all the other strips to the A/B base in this manner.

8. Carefully position the other A/B combination on top of the eight joined strips, and attach it with screws.

9. Drill ⅛" holes in the bottom for drainage. Ventilation may be added by drilling ¼" holes, 1" down from the top of every other cedar strip.

10. Sand all the edges.

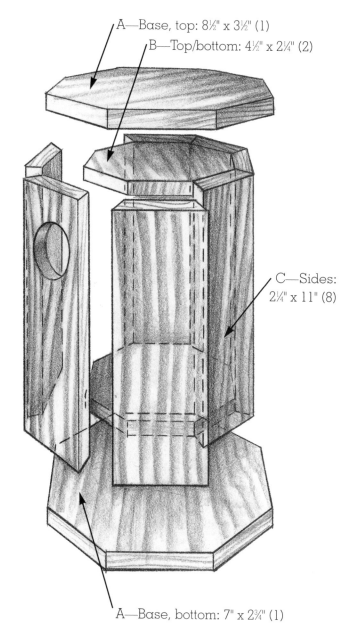

A—Base, top: 8½" x 3½" (1)

B—Top/bottom: 4½" x 2¼" (2)

C—Sides: 2¼" x 11" (8)

A—Base, bottom: 7" x 2¾" (1)

Bark and Moss Cottage

DESIGNER: **Susan Kinney**

What could be more pastoral than a moss- and bark-covered cottage? Simply decorate a purchased birdhouse with materials you gather on your next walk through the woods, and hang it on a covered porch.

Materials and Supplies

Wooden birdhouse, hanging style
Assortment of ⅛"- to ¼"-thick twigs
Evergreen sprig
Tree bark*

Sheet moss
Dried flowers
Gum eraser
White mohair yarn
Small photographs of room settings,
    cut from magazines
Piece of plastic wrap
Hot-glue gun and glue sticks
* *Of course, collect bark only from trees that have fallen to the ground…*

Tools

Scissors
Pruning shears

Instructions

1. Cut the sheet moss to size and glue it onto the roof.

2. Cut ¼"-thick twigs to trim the front of the roof and glue them in place.

3. Break the bark into small pieces, about 1" x 2", and glue them all over the front, sides, back, and bottom of the birdhouse. Glue four small pieces together to make a front stoop and glue it to the house. Glue the evergreen sprig and some dried flowers on either side of the front stoop.

4. Glue bark to the roof in the shape of dormers. Cut two magazine photographs showing room settings to size and glue them to the front of each window, then cover them with pieces of plastic wrap. Glue on ⅛"-thick twigs to frame in the window and decorate with sprigs of dried flowers.

5. To create the chimney, glue the gum eraser on one side of the roof peak, and glue on some yarn to create "smoke."

6. Break off small pieces of sheet moss and glue them in between the bark pieces so that none of the birdhouse wood shows.

TOWN HOUSE

DESIGNER: **CHRISTOPHER LAWING**

This elegant nest box may be a perfect fit for the sophisticated bird in your neighborhood.

CUT LIST

¼" pine plywood
 Front/back: 4⅜" x 16" (2)
 Sides: 4" x 12" (2)
 Floor: 4" x 4" (1)
 Roof: 5" x 5½" (1) and 5" x 5⅛" (1)

MATERIALS AND SUPPLIES

Balsa sheet, ³⁄₃₂" x 4"
Balsa trim, ¼" x ⅛" x 30"
Balsa trim, ⅛" x ⅛" x 30"
½" brads
2 brass hinges and screws, 1½" long
36-gauge copper sheet, 12" x 12",
 cut into 1½" x 6" strips
Carpenter's glue
Wine cork
Paintbrushes
Acrylic paints in off-white, green, taupe,
 and metallic gold

TOOLS

Circular saw or jigsaw
Drill with ⅜" and ¼" bits
Hammer
Craft knife
Screwdriver

INSTRUCTIONS

1. On the front and back pieces, measure down 4" from the top along both sides and cut to the midpoint to form the gables.

2. Drill a 1½" entrance hole on the front, centered, 10¾" from the bottom and 2³⁄₁₆" in from the side. Drill a ¼" mounting hole on the back of the house.

3. Assemble the sides, front, and back with brads.

4. Angle the ends of the roof pieces and nail them in place.

5. Drill holes in the bottom piece to match the holes in the hinges you selected, then mount one side of each hinge to the bottom. Drill matching holes on the floor-end of the front and back pieces, and mount the other side of the hinges. (These can be removed when you want to clean the box.)

6. Wrap the first copper strip around the roof eave. Cut and smooth to fit. Apply successive copper strips, overlapping each strip by ½". Fold the last strip so it covers the bottom of the roof. Cut a strip, 1½" x ½", and glue it to the left side of the roof to create a loop, into which you will insert the cork, painted gold.

7. Cut the ⅛" balsa trim to fit the outer sides of the front and glue it in place. Cut the ¼" trim so it is flush with the ⅛" trim in the front and flush with the sides along the back, and glue it in place. Cut and glue the ⅛" trim to the bottom of the gable (this will be the brace for the gable shingles).

8. Cut shingles from the balsa sheet in ½" x 1" strips. Begin the shingles by running them against the gable trim; glue them in place. Attach each successive row, overlapping them by ¼".

9. Cut a piece of copper for the door and position it on the front of the house. Cut ⅛" balsa trim to fit around the copper door and glue it onto the front. Cut more ⅛" trim for the windows and glue it in place. Cut balsa squares to fill in the windows and glue them on the house.

10. Apply at least two coats of paint to all surfaces and let dry.

VICTORIAN NUTHATCH HOUSE

DESIGNER: ROLF HOLMQUIST

The beauty of this nest box is that it combines mostly found materials in a way that is both rustic and elegant. Yours will be uniquely beautiful, too.

CUT LIST

Barn wood (or other found, weathered wood), about 1" thick

     Front/back: 6" x 9" (2)

     Sides: 4¾" x 6¼" (2)

     Floor: 4½" x 5" (1)

     Roof: 6½" x 8½" (2)

     Backboard: 4" x 15" (1)

MATERIALS AND SUPPLIES

Decking screws (no. 8)

Assorted old brass trim, hardware, screws, and "stuff"

Carpenter's glue

Wood putty

TOOLS

Saw

Jigsaw

Drill with ⅛" bit

Screwdriver

INSTRUCTIONS

1. Cut one end of the front and back pieces to a 45-degree angle.

2. On the front piece, drill a 1⅜"-wide entrance hole, centered, 6" up from the bottom.

3. Assemble the sides, front, back, and floor with screws.

4. Cut an 80-degree angle on the 6½" edge of both roof pieces so the peak joints meet evenly. Attach the roof pieces to the assembled box with screws.

5. Cut a sharp peak on the backboard. Drill a ¼" hole, centered, ½" below the peak. Attach the backboard to the back of the birdhouse with screws.

6. Glue and/or screw on the assorted brass fittings.

7. Weathered barn wood has a lot of cracks. To make the birdhouse less drafty, fill in the cracks with a generous amount of carpenter's glue. For large gaps, use wood putty.

CLEANING BIRDHOUSES

When the weather turns brisk and your birds have moved on, you should take some time to clean out your birdhouse. (Even if the birds are nonmigratory, the nesting season is over by late fall.) Birdhouses made so that the back, floor, top, or front, can be removed or opened are very useful. If your favorite birdhouse does not have this, you can take off one piece and refasten it with a hinge.

Cleaning birdhouses is really a simple matter: remove the nesting materials from the house, as well as any unwanted guests, such as mice, insects, and squirrels. If you do find insects, avoid using bug sprays unless absolutely necessary. Once the house is empty, scrub the inside with a stiff brush and soapy water. Take special care to rinse thoroughly. When your birds return in the spring, their home will be clean and ready for a new nest.

RUSTIC TITMOUSE HOUSE

DESIGNER: **GEORGE KNOLL**

Several species of birds are attracted to natural-looking birdhouses. Mount or hang this rustic log house near wooded land, and it may become home to a titmouse, a Carolina or black-capped chickadee, a nuthatch, or a downy woodpecker.

CUT LIST

Chunk of hardwood tree trunk or branch, about 6" to 8" wide and 9" long (wood shown here is walnut)

Slice of hardwood for roof, 6½" x 12"

MATERIALS AND SUPPLIES

2¼" decking screws

Wood glue

Wood shavings for woodpeckers

TOOLS

Band saw

Bench saw or handsaw

Jigsaw

Drill and ¼" bit

Screwdriver

INSTRUCTIONS

1. Saw the top of the wood chunk at an angle to create a sloped roof.

2. Use the band saw to saw out a cylinder from the center of the chunk.

3. Cut off a 1"-thick slice of wood from the cylinder to use as the base of the birdhouse. Drill four or five ¼" holes in the base for drainage.

4. Drill a 1¼" entrance hole about 6" to 8" up from the bottom. Cut at least two ⅝" ventilation notches anywhere near the top.

5. Glue and screw on the roof. Attach the bottom slice with two screws (no glue), so you can remove it for cleaning.

SOUTH AMERICAN GOURD HOUSE

DESIGNER: GINGER SUMMIT

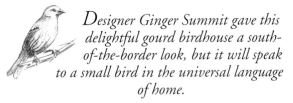

Designer Ginger Summit gave this delightful gourd birdhouse a south-of-the-border look, but it will speak to a small bird in the universal language of home.

MATERIALS AND SUPPLIES

Small, round, hardshell gourd, cured
Bleach
Rubber gloves
Large plastic dish pan or tub
Plastic or metal kitchen scrubbing pad
Brush with stiff, natural bristles
Compass with pencil
Sandpaper
Leather dyes in red, orange, light brown,
    and dark brown
Paintbrush
Exterior varnish, with u.v. inhibitor, if possible
Leather thong, 30" long

TOOLS

Dull kitchen knife
Drill with ¼" bit
Keyhole or hobby saw, motorized cutting tool,
    or small hand-held power jigsaw
Wood-burning tool

INSTRUCTIONS

1. Clean the gourd as described in step 1 of the Floral Gourd Birdhouse on page 22.

2. Cut the 1½" entrance hole, (see step 2, page 22).

3. Shake out the seeds and pulp through the hole, then sand the edge of the hole smooth.

4. Drill six small holes in the bottom of the gourd for drainage. Drill three holes at the top of the gourd for the leather thong.

5. Using the project photograph or other pictures, sketch your design onto the surface of the gourd.

6. Carefully, with light pressure, wood burn along the pencil lines.

7. Color in your design with leather dyes.

8. Protect the gourd with two coats of exterior varnish, letting each coat dry thoroughly.

9. Cut three 10"-long pieces of leather thong. Thread them through the holes at the top of the gourd and knot the ends together.

Rectilinear Birdhouse

DESIGNER: Robin Clark

Designer Robin Clark used redwood in straight, cleans lines, all pointing in the direction of a classically beautiful birdhouse.

Cut List

1" redwood*

    A: 7¼" x 7¼" (2)

    B: 3¼" x 9½" (2)

    C: 5½" x 9½" (2)

    D: 3⅞" x 9½" (2)

    E: 3⅞" x 3⅞" (1)

    F: 5¼" x 5¼" (1)

    G: 2½" x 9½" (2)

    H: 3¼" x 3¼" (1)

1" redwood is actually ¹¹⁄₁₆". If you use a thicker material, adjust these measurements.

Materials and Supplies

1¼" decking screws

Sandpaper

Tools

Table saw

Jigsaw

Drill with 1½" and ⅛" bits

Screwdriver

Instructions

1. Drill pilot holes, centered 1" from the top and bottom on pieces C and D. Drill pilot holes ⅜" from the edge and 1" down from each corner of the C pieces.

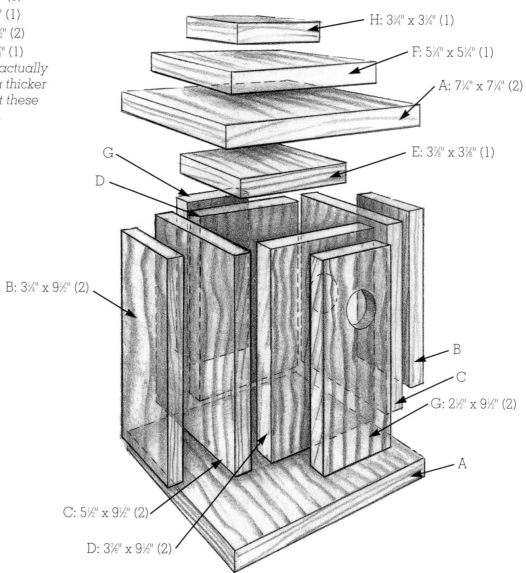

H: 3¼" x 3¼" (1)

F: 5¼" x 5¼" (1)

A: 7¼" x 7¼" (2)

E: 3⅞" x 3⅞" (1)

G

D

B: 3¼" x 9½" (2)

B

C

G: 2½" x 9½" (2)

A

C: 5½" x 9½" (2)

D: 3⅞" x 9½" (2)

2. Use screws to mount G, centered to D.

3. Mount B, centered, to C.

4. Drill a 1½" hole, centered 7" from the bottom on the G/D assembly that will be the front of the birdhouse. Cut off ¼" at the top of this assembly for ventilation.

5. On one A piece, drill three ⅛" pilot holes, centered 1⅜" from the sides. Using screws in the predrilled holes, mount the G/D assemblies between the wider B/C sides.

6. Position the body on the bottom by centering it on the square, with the entrance hole in the front, then secure with three screws.

7. Drill a ⅛" pilot hole in the center of F.

8. Drill two ⅛" pilot holes, centered, ¾" from the edge of H.

9. Draw a line connecting the two corners of F, then drill a ⅛" pilot hole, 2" in from each corner.

10. Center and attach E to A, and F to H (with the screw going through F into H, which will be the top).

11. Gently twist H until the pilot holes are visible, then, with F centered on A, screw them together, and return H to a squared position.

Note: The roof is designed to simply rest in the opening in the top, but it could be permanently attached with screws through A and into the sides.

12. Lightly sand all the edges.

Birds, such as the boat-tailed grackle (top) and the tufted titmouse (bottom), thrive in yards that combine woods, open space, and a variety of shrubs and flowers.

CAROLINA WREN HOUSE

DESIGNER: **ROBIN CLARK**

This classic design is a proven favorite with Carolina wrens. To attract other kinds of birds, simply modify the dimensions as indicated on the chart on page 125.

CUT LIST

1" cedar*

    A—Roof: 6¼" x 6½" (1)
    B—Back: 5⅜"* x 11¾" (1)
    C—Front: 4" x 8" (1)
    D—Floor: 4" x 4" (1)
    E—Sides: 4¹¹⁄₁₆"* x 10" (2)
    F—Toggles: ½" x ½" x 2¼" (2)

1" cedar stock is actually ¹¹⁄₁₆". If you use a thicker material, adjust these measurements.

On pages 50 to 61 you will find seven very different approaches to decorating this basic design.

Materials and Supplies

1¼" decking screws
Sandpaper

Tools

Circular or jigsaw
Drill with ⅛" and 1½" bits
Screwdriver
Router with ¼" round-over bit

Instructions

1. Bevel one end of A to a 15-degree angle. Drill ⅛" pilot holes, ⅞" from the side and 1¼" and 3¾" from the beveled end.

2. On B, centered ½" from the top and bottom, drill a ⅛" mounting hole and another pilot hole, 1⅜ from the bottom. Along each edge, ⅜" from the side and 3" from the top and bottom, drill four ⅛" pilot holes.

3. Drill a 1½" hole on C, centered, 6½" from the bottom.

4. On D, cut about ¼" from each corner.

5. On each E piece, cut a 15-degree angle on one end. Make sure each side is the same length, then drill a ⅛" pilot hole, ⅜" from the edge (1) centered on the square bottom and (2) 1¼" from the top of the short length on both side pieces.

6. On each toggle, drill a ⅛" pilot hole, ½" in from one end. Round the sides.

7. Use screws for all assembly. First, mount the bottom to the sides, keeping the sides flush to the back edge. Mount the back to the sides, allowing 1" spacing at the bottom. Mount the door to the sides, leaving about ¼" for ventilation. Attach the roof, making sure there is equal overhang on both sides. Finally, attach the toggles.

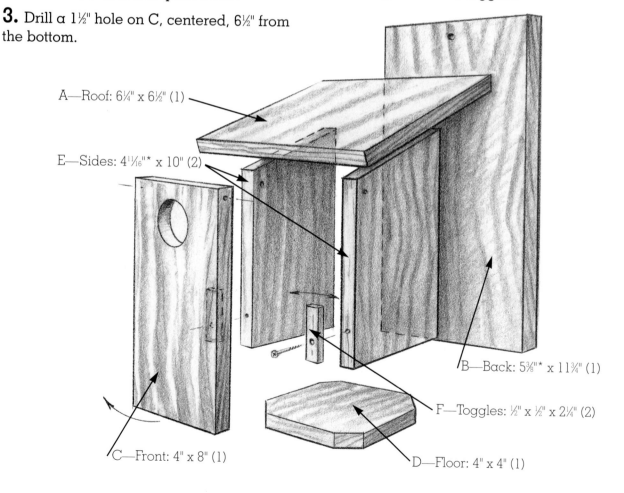

A—Roof: 6¼" x 6½" (1)

E—Sides: 4¹¹⁄₁₆"* x 10" (2)

B—Back: 5⅜"* x 11¾" (1)

F—Toggles: ½" x ½" x 2¼" (2)

C—Front: 4" x 8" (1)

D—Floor: 4" x 4" (1)

HOUSE WITH FAUX INLAID WOOD

DESIGN: DIANE WEAVER

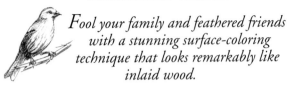

Fool your family and feathered friends with a stunning surface-coloring technique that looks remarkably like inlaid wood.

MATERIALS AND SUPPLIES

Carolina Wren House
Pencil
Metal ruler
Circle guide
Paintbrush (good quality) with fine point
Acrylic paints in black and yellow ocher
Walnut wood stain
Clear matte sealer

TOOLS

Craft knife

INSTRUCTIONS

1. Measure and mark the black lines first. Use the pencil to make light tick marks for the different dimensions that indicate the outside borders of the inlay graphic shapes. Use the craft knife and ruler to score the lines that outline these shapes. The first black line outlining the box is ⅛" thick. The inside black line is ½" away and of the same thickness. Mark and score the wood about 1⁄16" deep. Painting the lines will be easier and the line sharper because of the scoring.

2. Use the circle guide and pencil to mark the circle around the entrance hole, then draw the outer circle ½" away. Score these circles as you did the lines in step 1.

3. Divide the circle into eight equal sections and score the lines. To define the triangles within these sections, diagonally connect the corners of each section by scoring lines.

4. The diamond shapes are ½" from point to point. They are bisected at the center to divide the two shades of wood stain. Mark the diamond points and centers, starting with a triangle at the bottom outside corner of the birdhouse; work up, putting tick marks every ¼". Outline/score these shapes with the ruler and craft knife. Create all the diamonds in this manner. You may have to add a bar spacer to make your design work, so be sure to plan your pattern on paper ahead of time.

5. Mix up a very thin wash of yellow ocher and apply it to the entire house. The wash should be thin enough to look like a stain, but allow the wood grain to show through.

6. Mix the walnut stain well and apply a light coat to each diamond. When dry, apply a second coat to the top or left triangle inside the diamond. Apply two coats to the triangles in the circle.

7. Using the photograph as a guide, paint all the other black lines.

8. When the paint and stain are dry, apply a sealer to the entire house.

TUMBLING BLOCKS

DESIGNER: **MAGGIE ROTMAN**

Paint this popular American quilt pattern on your birdhouse, and keep a wren family warm and safe until the little ones fly away.

MATERIALS AND SUPPLIES

Carolina Wren House
Fine-grit sandpaper
Paintbrushes
Acrylic base coat
Ruler
Pencil
Acrylic paint in black and two contrasting
    colors of your choice

INSTRUCTIONS

1. Sand the birdhouse well, especially the edges of the front. (This will permit you to easily open and close the door when the area is built up with paint.)

2. Paint the outside of the birdhouse with the base coat and let dry.

3. Paint the outside of the birdhouse green or the color you want for the body of the house. Let dry and apply a second coat. Let dry.

4. Tumbling Blocks (also called Diamonds, Baby Blocks, and Stair Steps) is based on diamond shapes of contrasting light and dark colors that create a continuous, three-dimensional pattern. Draw the design on the roof and draw three diamonds down the front of the house.

5. Paint the design, using the photograph as a guide. Let dry.

PURPLE PASSION

DESIGNER: **PAT SCHIEBLE**

Simple sponging with carnival colors quickly and easily transforms this modest nest box.

MATERIALS AND SUPPLIES

Carolina Wren House

Acrylic paints in bright colors of your choice

Natural sponge

Grapevine tendrils

Hot-glue gun and glue sticks

TOOLS

Screwdriver

INSTRUCTIONS

1. Remove the toggles on the front of the birdhouse.

2. Sponge the body of the birdhouse in several complementary colors. Paint the roof and grapevine a contrasting color. Let dry.

3. Glue the grapevine to the front of the house, underneath the entrance hole.

WREN HOUSE WITH INCISED PATTERNS

DESIGN: **DIANE WEAVER**

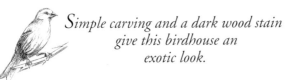

Simple carving and a dark wood stain give this birdhouse an exotic look.

MATERIALS AND SUPPLIES

Carolina Wren House
Ballpoint pen
Straightedge
Paintbrush
Sandpaper
Transfer paper
Walnut wood stain
Clean rag
Clear matte sealer
Mocha acrylic paint

TOOLS

Craft knife
V-shaped and curved wood-carving tools
Hand-held rotary power tool, fitted with
    a ¼" carbide cutter

INSTRUCTIONS

1. Trace the patterns onto the house using the transfer paper, the straightedge—where applicable—and the ballpoint pen. Apply enough pressure with the pen to lightly incise the wood, being careful not to go outside the pattern lines.

2. Use the straightedge and the craft knife to outline all the straight-line tracings, cutting about ⅟₁₆" into the wood. Then carefully cut the curves; lift the blade and reinsert the knife when a curve becomes too difficult. Cutting in this way will prevent the wood from splintering beyond the pattern area when you begin to carve.

3. For carving, use the v-shaped tool to remove most of the wood. If an area becomes too tight to get into with that tool, switch to the power tool. The power tool can also be used to smooth out your work; use the tip to carve out the berries. Use the curved carving tool to cut the shapes in the toggles that hold the front panel closed.

4. Apply the wood stain to the uncarved areas and let dry. Then apply the sealer to all the wood surfaces and let dry.

5. Apply the mocha paint in the carved areas. While the paint is still wet, use the rag to wipe some of it off and to clean up any paint outside the carved areas. When dry, apply a top coat of sealer.

ANGEL JEWEL HOUSE

DESIGNER: **SHELLEY LOWELL**

Here's a winsome box for storing love letters, jewelry, family snapshots, or other keepsakes (the dimensions are too small for housing most angels).

MATERIALS AND SUPPLIES

Carolina Wren House
Joint compound
Gesso
Fine-grit sandpaper
Damp cloth
Acrylic paints in colors of your choice
Paintbrushes
Multicolored jewels*
Craft glue
Self-hardening clay
2 small seashells
Angel sculpture (see step 9)
2 small brass hinges
Carpenter's glue
*available in crafts-supply stores

TOOLS

Phillips screwdriver

INSTRUCTIONS

1. Remove the toggles on the front of the house.

2. Fill all rough areas, cracks, and holes with joint compound. When dry, sand or wipe these areas down with a damp cloth until they are smooth.

3. Sand the sides of the front door and the inside of the birdhouse, where the door closes. (This will permit you to easily open and close the door when the area is built up with layers of paint.)

4. Gesso the entire birdhouse. You may have to sand again with fine sandpaper before putting on a second coat.

5. Paint the inside of the cabinet, using two coats of paint if necessary.

6. Draw your angels, hearts, and other patterns on the outside of the birdhouse. Paint the design and let dry.

7. Carefully glue on the jewels.

8. Apply two coats of water-based polyurethane to the entire outside of the house, allowing each coat to dry for 24 hours.

9. While you are waiting for the polyurethane to dry, try making an angel sculpture. This one was made from self-hardening clay, which, when dry, was sanded, coated with gesso, and painted. The wings were made with two small shells that were inserted into the clay when it was still pliable. You can also look for a ceramic angel or doll in a craft-supply store. Use carpenter's glue to secure the angel inside the entrance hole.

10. Attach the little brass hinges.

SAND-PAINTED BIRDHOUSE

DESIGNER: **CATHY SMITH**

The sand meanders on this distinctive birdhouse are, according to designer Cathy Smith, "energy spirals" associated with the bird goddess religion practiced by many ancient people, including Lithuanian and Minoan ancestors.

MATERIALS AND SUPPLIES

Carolina Wren House
Medium-grit sandpaper
Pencil
Paintbrushes, 1" flat bristle, #4 and #0 round
    sable or synthetic sable
Acrylic neutral gel*
Acrylic craft paint in turquoise
Acrylic matte finish varnish
Fine burnt orange craft sand, 4 to 7 ounces
Plastic applicator bottle
Toothpick
Spray acrylic matte finish
*made for mixing with paints to produce a
    translucent stain or pickling effect

INSTRUCTIONS

1. Sand the birdhouse to remove any splinters and to give the wood a little "tooth."

2. Mix a dab of turquoise paint with about 1 ounce of neutral gel. Apply *one* thin coat to all *outer* surfaces of the birdhouse, using the flat brush. Keep the strokes going in the same direction as the wood grain, and don't worry about perfect coverage. Let dry in a warm place.

3. Draw your meander patterns with pencil directly onto the painted surface. Use single lines, but leave enough space for ⅜" to ½" brush strokes—you will brush directly on top of the pencil lines. (The designer used square spirals in a random, asymmetrical pattern.) If you make mistakes while drawing, simply erase the lines; the sand is opaque and will cover them.

4. Working one section at a time, apply a thick coat of matte varnish over the pencil lines, using a #4 round brush for large spirals and the #0 brush for small ones. The varnish dries clear and flat, and serves as an adhesive for the sand. It is waterproof, too, so the sand will not dissolve when the birdhouse gets wet.

The varnish dries quickly so you will have only about 15 to 20 seconds in which to apply the sand. Apply the varnish as thickly as you can without having drips; the sand will soak it up. Apply the varnish to one small section, then pour on the sand. Overpouring is a good thing! Thump the birdhouse to remove the loose sand and recycle it back into the bottle.

Complete one side of the birdhouse at a time and allow the varnish/sand to dry completely before moving on to the next surface. If you make a mistake with the varnish and have sand stuck where you don't want it, correct the problem with a toothpick while still wet.

5. After you have applied one coat of varnish/sand to the pattern on all surfaces, repeat the entire procedure two to three more times. The more layers you apply, the more dimensional your pattern will be. Don't be concerned about sparse coverage on your first coat—that is to be expected. It takes at least two applications for complete coverage.

6. After all the layers are dry, spray the house with two to three coats of matte finish and let dry.

RECYCLED RETREAT

DESIGNER: **SHEILA A. SHEPPARD**

A remarkable combination of materials adds up to an unforgettably delightful birdhouse.

MATERIALS AND SUPPLIES

Carolina Wren House

Pencil

Metal ruler

Handles and wooden parts of old tools, such as a rake and shovel

Collection of pruned branches and twigs from maple, birch, or willow trees

Several square, hand-formed polymer clay loaves

Large rectangular baking dish

Oven parchment paper

2½" decking screws

White flat latex acrylic house paint

Paintbrush, stiff bristle

Medium-grit sandpaper

Assorted feathers

Leather thong, 8" long

Small brass bell

Flat-head brass tack

20-gauge jewelry wire, 6" long

TOOLS

Phillips-head screwdriver

Craft knife

¾" wood gouging or carving chisel

Drill and drill bits

Slicing blade

Miter saw with wood miter box or circular saw

Large table vise

INSTRUCTIONS

1. Remove the front panel of the birdhouse and the toggles that hold the panel in place. Save all the screws.

2. On the front panel, measure and mark a rectangle with 1"-wide sides. Use the craft knife to cut into the wood along the pencil lines to a depth of ⅛". Score between these lines with crosshatches.

3. Use your gouging tool to remove all the wood from the scored area to a depth of ⅛". Be sure the outer edge is clean. It is fine if the gouged area is slightly rough—this will allow the polymer clay to adhere better when it is baked.

4. Plan your inlay design. Slice ⅛" x 1" slabs off the square clay canes and arrange them in the grooved area to your satisfaction. Apply even pressure all around the inlay to be sure the sections fit together. Smooth out the surface and be sure all the clay reaches evenly inside the borders.

5. Lay the front panel, design side up, into a large baking dish, lined with parchment paper. Bake for 30 minutes in an oven, preheated to 275°. At this temperature, the wood will not burn (neither will the paper), but the clay will bond well to the roughened area. Remove from the oven and let cool.

6. While the panel is baking and cooling, assemble the wood tools to create a stand for the birdhouse. The designer miter-cut the

shovel handle so it would lie flat against, and also support, the longer lawn mower handle. Attach the various wooden pieces to the birdhouse, using decking screws (figure 1).

7. Place the toggles you removed in step 1 into a vise and drill about ½" down through the center vertically. Search your twig collection for two small, fan-shaped twigs. Apply glue to each end and insert the twigs into the holes.

8. Drill several holes in the top of the birdhouse and glue in some branches. Drill a hole in the front panel for a perch and glue in a small twig.

9. Reattach the front panel to the birdhouse. Screw on the toggles.

10. Mix a wash with the white paint. Brush the paint all over the birdhouse and the other wooden parts. When dry, use sandpaper to remove the paint if there is too much in any one area.

11. Add more paint to make the wash a little thicker and paint the branches and twigs. Let dry.

12. Tie several feathers together with the leather thong, add the bell, and attach the cluster to the side of the birdhouse with the brass tack. Use a piece of jewelry wire to attach a few feathers to the top branches.

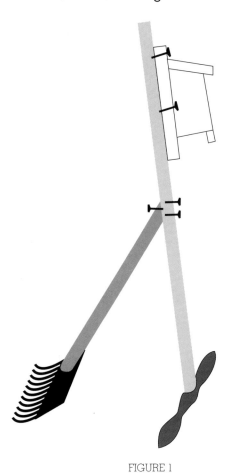

FIGURE 1

All birds, including the flicker (top) and the bluebird (bottom) require a water source near their nest.

Gourd Birdhouse and Feeder

DESIGNER: **Ginger Summit**

This beautifully decorated gourd set, with its wood burned bird motif, is bound to attract a variety of birds, and will look very attractive hanging in your yard.

Materials and Supplies

2 hardshell gourds, cured, 12" to 16"
Bleach
Rubber gloves
Large plastic dish pan or tub
Plastic or metal kitchen scrubbing pad
Brush with stiff, natural bristles
Compass with pencil
Sandpaper
Leather dyes in leaf green, light brown,
    and dark brown
Curly twig to use for a perch
Waxed linen
Tapestry needle
Leather thong, 12" to 14" long
Paintbrush
Exterior varnish, with u.v. inhibitor, if possible

Tools

Serrated spoon, such as a grapefruit spoon
Dull kitchen knife
Drill with ⅛" and ¼" bits
Keyhole or hobby saw, motorized cutting tool,
    or small hand-held power jigsaw
Wood-burning tool

Instructions

1. Clean the gourds as described in step 1 of the Floral Gourd Birdhouse on page 22.

2. Cut the 1½" entrance hole (see step 2 on page 22).

Making the birdhouse

3. Shake out the seeds and pulp through the hole and sand the edge of the hole smooth.

4. Drill three small holes in the bottom of the gourd for drainage. Drill a hole on each side of the neck of the gourd for the leather thong.

Making the feeder

5. Sketch the areas on the gourd that you want to cut. Use the sharp knife to make a small slit along one of the lines. Insert your cutting tool and carefully cut out the area. (*Tip:* If you use a power tool, make sure the gourd is secure on your work surface. A foam pad will help keep the gourd from slipping.)

6. Remove the seeds and pulp; most will come out by hand. Use the serrated spoon to remove the remaining material. Sand the cut edges smooth.

7. Complete step 4.

Decorating the birdhouse and the feeder

8. Using the project photograph or other pictures, sketch leaves and birds onto the surface of the gourds.

9. Carefully, with light pressure, wood burn along the pencil lines. Use the leather dyes to color in your design.

10. Protect the gourds by applying two coats of varnish, allowing each coat to dry.

11. Thread the leather thong through the holes at the top of the gourds and knot the ends.

12. Drill five or six ⅛" holes around the entrance hole on the birdhouse and use the waxed linen to sew the twig to the gourd.

Diad Birdhouse

Designer: Thomas Stender

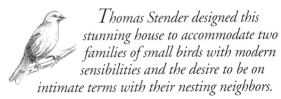

Thomas Stender designed this stunning house to accommodate two families of small birds with modern sensibilities and the desire to be on intimate terms with their nesting neighbors.

Cut List

Glue forms: scrap 2 x 4s—5 pieces 16" long, 5 pieces 12" long

⅜" lauan plywood

Floors: 3³⁄₁₆" x 7¾" (2)

Sides: 4⅝" x 7¾" (2)

¹⁄₁₆" mahogany or maple veneer

Front: 7" x 14" (6)

Roof: 6" x 14" (6)

Perches: hardwood, ⁵⁄₁₆" x ⁵⁄₁₆" x 6½" (2)

Chimney: pine or similar, ½" x 1¼" x 1¼" (1)

Materials and Supplies

Tracing paper

Pencil

Ruler

Sheet of paper

Rubber cement

Epoxy glue

Rubber gloves

Sandpaper

Thin plastic sheeting

Builder's square

Compass

Adjustable bevel

Paintbrush

Varnish

1" decking screws (no. 6)

3p finishing nails

Tools

Band saw

Table saw

Low angle block plane

Drill press

Dozuki saw or small backsaw

Cabinetmaker's rasp

Chisels

Pilot bit with countersink to match screws

Drill and ⅛" bit

Clamps

Screwdriver

Note: This is a relatively advanced project because the construction requires laminating and fitting curved pieces. In practice, however, a competent woodworker with a lot of patience will be able to build the birdhouse. Because the curved pieces will not exactly match the curves as drawn, the designer has included only major dimensions and even these are not sacred. Building proceeds by fitting new pieces to those already made— an effective woodworking practice for any project. Please read all the instructions carefully before beginning this project.

Instructions

Building the twin houses

1. The project consists of two identical birdhouses glued together with a chimney covering the roof intersection. Do not glue the roofs to the walls prematurely.

Start by gluing 2 x 4s or plywood together to make 3½" x 7½" x16" and 3½" x 7½" x 14" blocks for the gluing forms. If your band saw is limited to 6", use that dimension and position the laminate layers very carefully. Study figures 1 and 2 to understand the curves and measurements of the laminated pieces. Enlarge figure 1 on a copier to full size and trace the full-size curves for the roof and curved side/front onto two pieces of paper. Rubber cement these to the narrow faces of the blocks at an angle that maximizes the area of the pressing surfaces. The outside of the curve should not be closer than ½" to the outside of the block. Extend the copied lines in fair curves to the edges of the block. Take a minute to make sure that your

band saw is cutting straight and square. Band saw smoothly to the line. (If you are not using a ½" x 3T hook tooth blade, try one.) The roof and side/front are thin enough that no thickness allowance is necessary.

2. Bend the veneer to determine which direction deflects more readily. Stack and mark 3 pieces per sandwich so that the "bendy way" matches the form. The grain in the side/fronts runs vertically (across the curve) to accommodate the 2" radius, so use

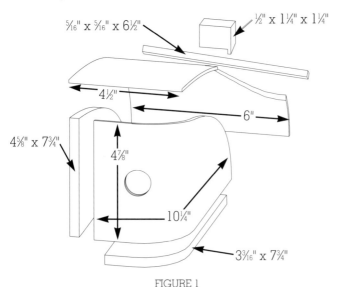

⁵⁄₁₆" x ⁵⁄₁₆" x 6½"

½" x 1¼" x 1¼"

4½"

6"

4⅝" x 7¾"

4⅞"

10¼"

3³⁄₁₆" x 7¾"

FIGURE 1

veneer with no cracks or obvious weaknesses. Two pieces of plastic sheet outside the glued sandwich release the sandwich from the gluing form. Try to keep wrinkles out of the plastic. You might try yellow glue for these laminations if the houses will never go outdoors, but you are likely to find that it is too flexible to maintain the desired shape. Epoxy produces a stronger and more rigid glue line.

Glue and clamp one sandwich at a time. Roll or spread slightly thickened epoxy onto both surfaces of each glue line to prevent starved joints; (you need 3 pieces of veneer per sandwich, which means 2 glue lines and 4 glued surfaces). As you clamp the sandwich inside the mold, keep the mold pieces aligned. This will require clamping lengthwise as well as across the thickness of the form. Don't let the clamps deform the sandwich and don't skimp on clamps. Wait patiently at least six hours. Repeat for the other curved pieces.

3. From this point on, it is a good idea to mark and keep together the pieces for each house. Trim the outboard long edges of the roof pieces straight and square to the curve. Use the gluing form for orientation. Check for squareness by standing the roof on its trimmed edge on a flat surface. Gauge with a square at several places along the outside of the curve. Rip the other long edges oversize. Trim the bottom edges of the

5¹⁄₁₆"

12¼"

4⅞"

8⅛"

10¹⁄₁₆"

FIGURE 2

side/fronts similarly. Bore a 1" hole through the front, centered both ways on the outside of the front.

4. Rip the ⅜" plywood to width (3³⁄₁₆" or so) for the floors and cut one end square, allowing extra length. Trace each side/front curve onto its floor, holding the long side against the edge of the floor and the short side aligned with the squared end. This will likely require bending the side/front by hand, so clamp the floor to your bench top. Band saw to the line. Fasten the side/front to the bottom with two screws on the front and two small finishing nails snipped to ¾" long into ample pilot holes through the side. If you do not plan to put the birdhouse outdoors, simply glue each side/front to its bottom, carefully aligning the bottom edges.

5. Cut two pieces of ⅜" plywood oversize, about 5" x 7", making sure that two edges are square. The side goes behind the front and outside the bottom. Make sure that the side is square with the bottom. Fasten these pieces with two screws. (For indoor use, glue the square edges to the front and bottom.)

6. With the dozuki saw and a block plane, trim the end of the front flush with the side. Trace the inside curve of each roof onto its plywood side, making certain that this cutting line does not miss the bottom and the front. Band saw to the line. Check the fit between the roof and sides and adjust if necessary. The outside of the roof extends ½" past the plywood side.

7. To make sure that you will be able to remove the bottom of the house in order to

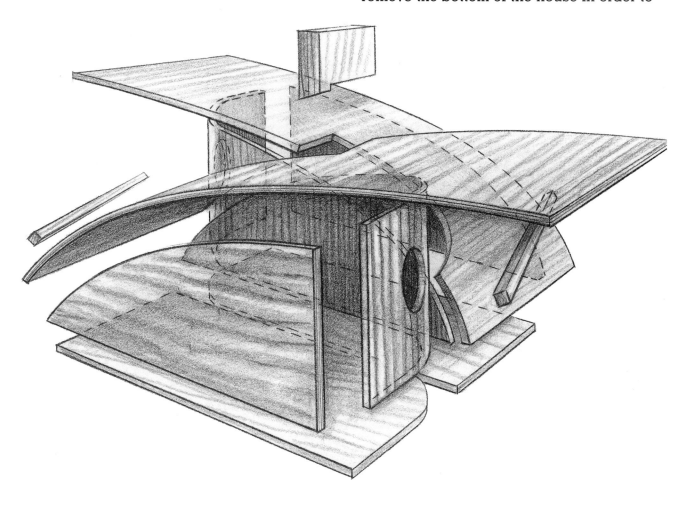

69

clean it, clamp the sides to a block the same length as the bottom is wide to maintain the shape of the house. Remove the four screws and rotate the bottom until it clears the plywood side. The finishing nails remain in place. You may have to relieve the top outboard edge of the bottom. Reassemble. Use epoxy to attach one roof to its house. Trim the back of the roof flush with the bottom.

Fitting the roofs to the adjoining houses

8. (*Warning:* This step takes longer to describe than to do!) Begin with the glued roof. The roof should run just below the hole in the adjoining house front. Transfer the height of the bottom of the hole to the outside of the roof. This is a vertical measurement, not along the outside of the curve. From that point, pencil a square across the roof. Draw another straight line where the roof will be trimmed flush with its own house. Draw a third line, parallel to the second line and $\frac{1}{2}$" outside of it, extended to the front of the roof. Position the two houses parallel with each other and offset so that a straightedge held against the front of the adjoining house hits the squared line on the back of the glued roof. Working on a grid surface will aid this operation. Use a square to mark the area where the two roofs will intersect. With a compass, held vertically and always square to the lengthwise direction of the houses, transfer the side/front curve of the adjoining house to the glued roof. With the bottom of the assembled house held firmly on the band saw table, saw somewhat outside of these lines (the offset will depend on your self-assurance today!). Now trim carefully toward the lines, constantly checking the fit between the glued roof and the adjoining house, until the side/fronts of the two houses meet and the roof runs just under the hole.

9. Glue the remaining roof to its house and fit the second roof as you did the first. Cut the backs of the roofs even with the outside of the holes and trim the fronts of the roofs to an overhang that looks good to you. When you are pleased with yourself or have adjusted to the obvious unpredictability of geometry, epoxy the side/fronts of the houses together.

10. Use an adjustable bevel to find the angles of the roof tops in the area where they meet. Mark these angles on opposite sides of the chimney piece, beginning about 1" from the top. Square the ends of those lines across the faces. Saw the angled lines to $\frac{1}{8}$" from the opposite side. Fit and epoxy in place.

11. The end of each $\frac{5}{16}$"-square perch is glued to the roof at an angle that provides bird clearance below and outside of the hole in the adjoining front. You may wish to ease the corners of the perches, but be wary of making them look like cheap chopsticks. Mark their positions on the roofs using an adjustable bevel and ruler to transfer one mark to the other roof. Cover the marks when you epoxy the perches in place. Trim one end of the perch flush with the roof edge and the other even with the roof edge and the outside of the hole.

12. Apply one or two coats of varnish to all the wood surfaces. Stain the chimney as you like, and let dry.

BLUEBIRD CATHEDRAL
DESIGNER: GEORGE HARRISON

This gorgeous cypress cathedral will provide nesting bluebirds with a truly inspirational place to raise their young.

CUT LIST

1" cypress

    A: 11½" x 15" (1)
    B: 4" in diameter (1)
    C: 11" x 6" (2)
    D: 6" x 12" (1)
    E: 11" x 6" (2)
    F: 12" x 13½" (1)
    G: 2½" x 6" (6)

MATERIALS AND SUPPLIES

2" decking screws
2" brads
Wood glue
Wood putty
Sandpaper

TOOLS

Table saw
Jigsaw
Screwdriver
Hammer

INSTRUCTIONS

1. Cut two 45-degree angles on one 6" side of D to form the peak on the back piece.

2. Cut a 45-degree angle on one 11" side of *both* E pieces.

3. Use screws to attach D to both E pieces. (You can unscrew the back when you need to clean out the nest box.)

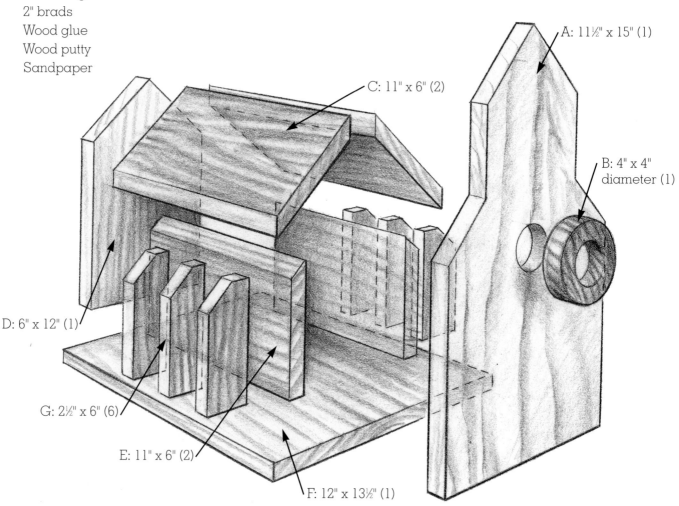

C: 11" x 6" (2)

A: 11½" x 15" (1)

B: 4" x 4" diameter (1)

D: 6" x 12" (1)

G: 2½" x 6" (6)

E: 11" x 6" (2)

F: 12" x 13½" (1)

4. Cut 45-degree angles on both 6" sides of the two C pieces.

5. Use brads to attach the roof sections to the sides.

6. Mark and measure 8" up on both 15" sides of A. Cut 45-degree angles on both sides. Mark and measure 4" above the angled cut and cut two more 45-degree angles on each side. The width at the top of A should be 7½".

7. Cut a 1½" entrance hole in A, centered, 7½" from the bottom.

8. Cut a 1½"-diameter hole in B. Glue B over the entrance hole in A, then fasten with brads.

9. Use brads to attach A to the assembled roof, sides, and back.

10. Fasten the base to the assembled box by nailing brads from the bottom.

11. Cut a 45-degree angle on one 2½" side (leave ½" with no angle) on all six G pieces. Glue the six buttresses in place, equally spaced on the base. Screw them to the base from the bottom.

12. Fill all nail holes with wood putty. When dry, sand the entire birdhouse.

PROTECTING YOUR TENANTS

Once birds come to nest near your house, you have a responsibility to discourage unwanted guests, such as snakes, rodents, squirrels, and insects. Baby birds and eggs are particularly susceptible to predators. (Both are delicacies for raccoons and squirrels.)

The best way to prevent predators from jeopardizing birds is to provide a birdhouse with the proper dimensions (see the chart on page 125). For instance, making sure the entrance hole is the right size for the birds you want to attract, and thus too small for raccoons and squirrels, helps protect the rightful occupants. Attaching a metal piece that has been cut to fit around the hole will keep squirrels from chewing their way in; framing the entrance hole with a 1-inch block of wood helps deter raccoons. Because cats and raccoons do not like getting grease on their fur, try smearing axle grease on the birdhouse post.

When you mount a birdhouse, be sure it is at least 5 feet from the ground. A cylinder of sheet metal attached to the pole 18 inches from the ground, with the metal extending 10 inches from the pole on all sides, will discourage cats, squirrels, and raccoons. If cats are a problem, avoid mounting your feeders and birdbaths near shrubs or other areas where cats might hide or near trees or surfaces from which cats could leap. If you find insects in the birdhouse, make sure you use a bug spray that is safe for birds. If you find wasps, coat the inside of the house with bar soap.

Nesting birds also face danger from other birds. Starlings and some sparrows often drive away songbirds, take over their nests, and even build nests over the other bird's eggs. If you have this problem and have a house with a perch, remove it, as the perch is largely decorative and may attract unwanted birds.

One last note: many birds are injured by flying into windows; they see sky and trees reflected in the window and mistake it for open space. You can prevent this by putting up a screen, nonreflective window coating, or flash tape on the outside of the window, or by planting trees or shrubs nearby to cut down on window reflection. You can also place a bird feeder close to the window to slow birds down.

CRIMSON GOURD BIRDHOUSES

DESIGNER: HAL HALL

These brightly painted gourds are just the right size for attracting wrens and chickadees. Hang two or three in a tree or from hooks on your front porch.

MATERIALS AND SUPPLIES

Hardshell gourd, cured
Gourd scraps
Bleach
Rubber gloves
Large plastic dish pan or tub
Plastic or metal kitchen scrubbing pad
Brush with stiff, natural bristles
Sandpaper
Compass with pencil
Paintbrushes
Wood stains, leather dyes, acrylic paints,
     and/or water-based marking pens
Wood glue
Exterior varnish, with u.v. inhibitor, if possible
Leather thong, 12" long

TOOLS

Drill with ¼" bit
Keyhole or hobby saw, motorized cutting tool,
     or small hand-held power jigsaw
Wood-burning tool

INSTRUCTIONS

1. Clean the gourd as described in step 1 of the Floral Gourd Birdhouse on page 22.

2. Cut the 1" entrance hole (see step 2 on page 22) high enough up the side that the bird can step down into the nest.

3. Shake out the seeds and pulp through the hole, then sand the edge of the hole smooth.

4. Drill three small holes in the bottom of the gourd for drainage. Drill a hole on each side of the neck of the gourd for the leather thong.

5. Using a pencil, draw a pleasingly curved horizontal line around the gourd to separate it into two areas. If you desire, you can wood burn that line, as well as other lines and patterns. Allow the shape of the gourd and its particular surface qualities to suggest how to embellish it.

6. Color the gourd with wood stains, acrylic paints, leather dyes, and/or water-based marking pens.

7. Glue on a scrap of gourd to create a roof and another to make a perch.

8. Apply two coats of varnish, allowing each coat to dry thoroughly.

9. To create a hanger, thread the leather thong through the holes in the gourd's neck and tie the ends together.

EMERALD CITY

DESIGNER: **PAT SCHIEBLE**

To discourage the local wrens from nesting in the hanging baskets on her back porch, designer Pat Schieble pulled out all the stops (and every scrap of molding she could find!) and created an extravaganza worthy of Oz.

Materials and Supplies

Simple wooden birdhouse*
Molding and picture frame scraps**
Miscellaneous wood scraps
Assorted metal knickknacks
Sandpaper
Hot-glue gun and glue sticks
Length of old gold chain-link necklace
Drapery pole finial
Imitation clock face
Acrylic spray paint: emerald green, yellow,
    and gold
Clear acrylic spray
*You can make a simple birdhouse or buy one.
Make sure it has a bottom attached with
screws so you can clean the birdhouse after
the birds have grown and flown away.
**Ask your local home-supply store for scraps
and discontinued samples.

Tools

Miter box
Saw
Drill with ⅛" bit

Instructions

1. Saw the scraps into pieces of varying lengths and sand any rough edges.

2. Glue the scraps to the birdhouse. Although you may want to use the photograph to guide you, the final look of this birdhouse will depend on your materials and imagination! As you work, step back from time to time to evaluate your progress. In the case of this birdhouse, more is better! Keep gluing on scraps until you are satisfied.

3. Glue on the drapery pole finial and the assorted metal details.

4. Saw a piece of wood for the drawbridge. Drill two holes in one end and thread two pieces of chain-link necklace through the holes; glue to secure. Glue the drawbridge in place and then glue the ends of the necklace to each side of the entrance hole.

5. Spray the entire birdhouse green. When dry, lightly spray some areas with gold paint. Paint the drawbridge with yellow paint to create the famous yellow bricks.

6. When dry, spray the birdhouse with clear acrylic and let dry.

TEACUP BIRDHOUSES

DESIGNER: **TERRY TAYLOR**

Designer Terry Taylor transformed a pair of terra-cotta birdhouses into an excuse for a tea party by creating a mosaic roof with flea market teacups. Cream and sugar, Mrs. Wren, or just a little lemon?

MATERIALS AND SUPPLIES

Terra-cotta birdhouse*
Assorted china plates, cups, and saucers
Thin-set cement mortar
Sanded floor grout
Containers for mixing mortar and grout
Rubber or latex gloves
Polyethylene packing sheet foam
Sponge
Lint-free rags
Protective sealant (optional)
Available from garden centers and craft-supply stores; they come in the traditional reddish color and sometimes in the off-white color pictured here.

TOOLS

Tile nipper
Safety glasses
Palette knife or small spatula

INSTRUCTIONS

1. Use tile nippers (while wearing safety glasses) to cut irregular pieces from the rims of your plates, striving to preserve the edges of the plates. Set these aside to use on the edge of the roof.

2. Continue to cut the plates into small pieces, about 1" in size. Set all of these pieces aside.

3. Carefully, use tile nippers to separate the handles from your chosen cups. This is best done by placing the tile nipper about ½" away from the handle. Don't fret if your handles break apart. It takes practice to keep the handle intact. If at first you don't succeed…

4. Mix a small amount of cement mortar, according to the manufacturer's directions. Mix the dry mortar into about ⅓ cup of water until you have the consistency of thick mud. Apply mortar to the edge of the birdhouse roof. Use the plate edge pieces to finish the roof edge. Cut more edge pieces if needed, but one plate's worth should do.

5. Apply mortar to the rest of the roof. If you are using cup handles, position them first. Add a little mortar to the base of the handle to help it fit well onto the roof. Continue to place small pieces onto the roof. Leave about ¼" or less between each piece, cutting fill-in pieces as needed. Allow the finished roof to dry for at least 24 hours.

6. Mix the sanded floor grout into about ¼ cup of clean water, according to the manufacturer's directions, until you achieve the consistency of cake frosting. Use a small square of polyethylene foam to apply the grout to the roof of the birdhouse. Wear latex gloves to protect your hands. Work the grout into the spaces between your plate pieces. Cover the entire roof in this manner. After about 15 minutes, begin removing excess grout and grout haze with clean pieces of the foam, a barely damp sponge, or lint- free rags. If your birdhouse has a small hole for hanging, use a nail to clean the excess grout from the hole.

7. Allow the birdhouse to dry, following the manufacturer's directions for curing the grout. If you wish, you may give your birdhouse additional protection by coating it with a protective sealant compatible with your grout.

Noah's Ark Birdhouse

Designer: **Christi Hensley**

Two by two, those little eggs will have a charming place to hatch. (Coming or going, this birdhouse has unforgettable views!)

Cut List

¾" pine

    Front/back: 5½" x 5½" (2)

    Side: 7" x 3½" (2)

    Roof A: 7½" x 11" (1)

    Roof B: 7" x 11" (1)

    Floor: 7" x 3¼" (1)

¼" dowel, 3" long

Materials and Supplies

1½" brads
1½" decking screws
Wood glue
Sandpaper
Paintbrushes
White acrylic primer
Pencil
Acrylic paints in sky blue, red, gray, white,
    green, yellow, pink, and black
Wood stain
Clear polyurethane

Tools

Table saw
Band saw
Jigsaw
Drill with ⅛" and ¼" bits
Hammer
Screwdriver

Instructions

1. Nail the roof pieces together so that Roof A overlaps Roof B.

2. Trim off one corner on both the front and back, so each has one side that measures 3½".

3. Drill a 1⅜" entrance hole, centered, in the front piece. About ½" below this hole, drill a ¼" hole, and glue in the dowel.

4. Cut 45-degree angles on both 7" sides of the floor.

5. Attach the front and back to the floor with screws.

6. Cut a 45-degree angle on the 7" edge of each side piece. Attach the sides to the floor with screws. (There will be an opening between the sides and the roof for ventilation.)

7. Nail the roof onto the house, leaving a 3½" overhang in front.

8. Sand the birdhouse.

9. Apply a coat of primer and let dry.

10. Using the photograph as a guide, sketch the animals onto the front, back, and roof. Feel free to add your own design elements. Paint the design and let dry.

11. Stain the edges of the unpainted wood and let dry.

12. Apply two coats of polyurethane, letting each coat dry thoroughly.

POSTMODERN BIRDHOUSE

DESIGNER: **THOMAS STENDER**

This delightful temple is perfect for spiritually inclined birds that seek a more practical floor plan than those ancient models.

CUT LIST

⅜" lauan plywood
>   Sides: 7¾" x 6" (2)
>   Front/back: 3¾" x 6" (2)

Base: ½" lauan plywood, 8½" x 11¾" (1)

Columns: ⅝" dowels, 6¼" long (10)

Perch: pine, ⅞" x 1½" x 2" (1)

MATERIALS AND SUPPLIES

Sheet copper or aluminum (heavy flashing),
>   9" x 12"

Ruler and pencil or large compass

Sheet of heavyweight paper

Scissors

Wood glue

Clamps

Sandpaper

Structural epoxy, thickened with microfibers,
>   if possible

Acrylic paints (optional)

Paintbrush

Bag of dried beans

Decking screws

Small copper nails

TOOLS

Table saw

Coping saw

Band saw (optional)

Low angle block plane or fine rasp

Brace with 1¼" and ⅝" bits

Tin snips

Pilot bit with countersink to match screws

Drill with ⅛" bit

Screwdriver

INSTRUCTIONS

1. Cut the plywood pieces to size. Mark and bore the 1¼" entrance hole centered in both directions in one end piece. Back up or drill from both sides to avoid splitting out.

2. Using a ruler and pencil or a large compass, draw an arc with a radius of 10" on a piece of heavy paper. Draw the arc at least 9" long. Carefully cut along the line with scissors. Use this template to draw the roof line on one of the ends. Make sure that the roof line is balanced by measuring the long edges of the house end. Clamp the ends together and use a coping saw to cut the roof line. Fair the curve with a low angle block plane or fine rasp, being careful to keep the edges square with the surfaces. *If you have a band saw with enough capacity, glue the four pieces of the house together, then mark and saw the roof line.*

3. Clamp the four pieces of the house together in their final positions. Use the paper template to extend the roof line onto the ends of the sides. Mark the inside and outside top edges of the sides. Unclamp and plane the top edges of the sides to the lines.

4. Screw the sides to the back end.

5. Mark and bore holes for the dowels, ¼" deep, through the base. Back up as usual. Try to use a bit that closely matches the dowels.

6. Cut the 19-degree angle at the top ends of the columns, but leave the columns long for now. Remember that the columns go through the base. If you are working on a table saw, cut ten 6" dowels. Then cut the angle on two columns and check their angle and length with the house and base preassembled. Clamp a stop to your saw's miter gauge at the adjusted distance and trim all the angled ends on the dowels.

7. Cut out the perch block and plane the top to the same radius as the roof line.

8. At this point, you can paint the wood pieces, if you wish. (For best effect, paint with contrasting colors. If you try to imitate a Greek temple too closely, you will risk ruining the joke, such as it is.) Do not finish any surfaces that will be glued.

9. Preassemble the pieces to make sure the roof will lie nicely on the house and columns.

Prebend the roof by rolling it loosely around a large cylinder, such as a large plastic pipe. Mark the position of the house.

10. Glue the house in place on the base, then the perch. Glue the columns into their holes; if possible, use a structural epoxy, thickened with microfibers. Remember to align the angles as accurately as you can. Clean up the bottom of the base.

11. Put the roof in place, mark all glue areas, and rough these areas with

sandpaper or a file. Spread a thin layer of epoxy on the tops of the house and columns and allow to harden. Spread another layer of epoxy over the first layer and place the roof in position. Weight it down with a bag of dried beans. To make the roof truly weather-worthy, drill pilot holes through the copper sheeting and drive small copper nails through the holes and into the tops of the columns. Either way, epoxy the top first to make drilling and driving easier.

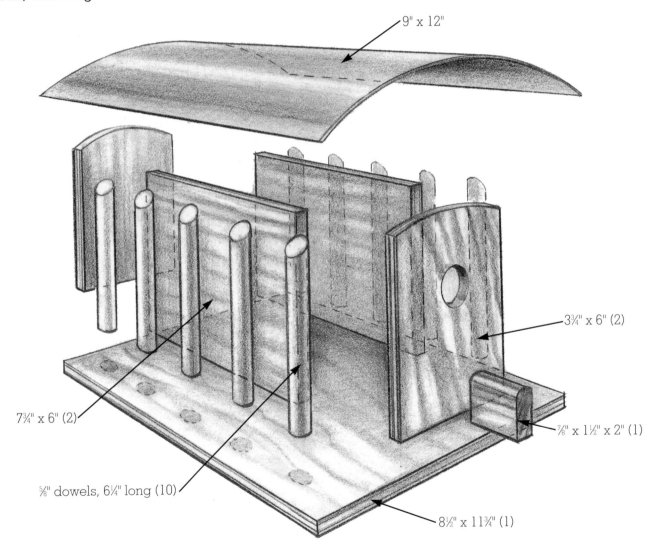

9" x 12"

3¾" x 6" (2)

7¾" x 6" (2)

⅝" dowels, 6¼" long (10)

⅞" x 1½" x 2" (1)

8½" x 11¾" (1)

SMALL SONGBIRD ROOST BOX

DESIGNER: **DON STEVENSON**

Designer Don Stevenson re-created this remarkable 1840s Carolina wood-fired tobacco barn to provide shelter for small, northern dwelling songbirds. Mount it eight to ten feet off the ground or on a tree or building where it will receive a lot of sun and not much wind. You just might see tufted titmice, black-capped and Carolina wrens, chickadees, nuthatches, or bluebirds, flying in to enjoy a respite from the cold.

CUT LIST

¾" fir

     A1: Front—7¼" x 13" (1)

     A2: Back—7¼" x 13" (1)

     B: Sides—5½" x 10" (2)

     C: Shed roof anchor—1¼" x 4" x 4 (1)

½" exterior plywood

     D: Floor—5½" x 5½" (1)

     E: Base—8" x 13" (1)

¼" exterior plywood

     F1: Barn roof, left—6½" x 9" (1)

     F2: Barn roof, right—6¼" x 9" (1)

     G: Shed roof—6¾" x 9" (1)

     H: Barn vent backing—1" x 1" (2)

Interior closure jambs: ¾" plywood, 1" x 12"

Shed roof posts: hardwood limb, about ⅜" x 4" (2)

Split firewood: hardwood limb, about 1" x 18" (1)

Shed roof brace: oak, ⅜" x ⅜" x 3½" (2)

Barn fireplace: oak, ½" x 2 x 1¾" (1)

Barn entrance door:

     Base—³⁄₃₂" paneling, 1¼" x 2⅝"

     Face boards—oak, ¹⁄₁₆" x ⅜" x 2⅝" (1)

     Trim—³⁄₁₆" x ⅜" x 12" (random length)

Barn vent trim: oak, ⅛" x ¼" x 6" (random length)

Hardwood dowel, ½" x 7" (3)

Board and batten siding: oak, 4/4 or 3/4 x 40',
re-sawn as described in steps 17 and 18

¾" treated yellow pine

     Roof shingles: 5½" x 20'*

*The ¾" stock is re-sawn to ⅜" x 1½" x random
lengths to accommodate splitting the 700
shingles, each ¹⁄₁₆" x ⅜" x 1½". See steps 21
and 22.*

MATERIALS AND SUPPLIES

3d finish nails

4d finish nails

20-gauge brads, ½" long

18-gauge brads, ¾"' long

Decking screws, no. 8

Carpenter's glue

Wood filler

Vinyl caulk

Exterior latex paint in black, white, orange,
     yellow, dark blue, and red

Paintbrushes, 1" flat bristle and ⅜" stencil brush

TOOLS

Drill with ¼" and ½" bits

Scroll saw

Table saw

Band saw

Jigsaw

Motorized cutting tool with 18- and 20-gauge
     drill bits

Sanding block or belt sander

Wood vice

Clamps

Phillips screwdriver

Hammer

INSTRUCTIONS

1. Mark the vertical centerline on A1 to
locate the center of the roof peak. Mark the
three ½" dowel holes as indicated in figure 1.

2. Place A1 exactly on top of A2. Nail them
together, leaving ⅛" of the nail heads
protruding so that you can remove the nails
in step 3. A1 will be your template for cutting
and drilling both boards.

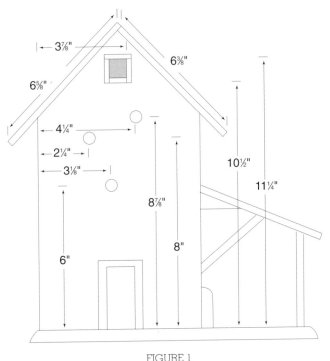

FIGURE 1

3. Cut the two 45-degree angles on both boards to create the roof pitch. Drill the three dowel holes through both boards. Remove the nails.

4. Drill the center out of the ¾" x ¾" square barn vent near the top of both A pieces. Use a scroll or coping saw for the inside cut.

Making the front door

5. Mark the location of the 1¼" x 2⅝" front door on A1. Assemble the door using the ³⁄₃₂" x 1¼" x 2⅝" paneling as backing board upon which you glue the three ¹⁄₁₆" x ⅜" x 2⅝" oak door boards vertically. (Leave tiny spaces between these boards.) Check the door for square and plumb.

6. Place the door over the layout lines and, if necessary, sand the edges square. Nail the door in place using 20-gauge brads. Fill the nail holes with wood filler, and wipe or sand off the excess. Wipe away any excess glue. When dry, glue the trim boards in place, then predrill holes using a 20-gauge drill bit, and nail them with 20-gauge brads.

7. Shape the door handle from a piece of ⅛" x ⅛" oak, about 3" long. The finished size should be ¹⁄₁₆" x ⅛" x ⅜". Nail and glue the door handle in place.

8. Glue and nail one of the vent backing pieces onto the inside of A1 to cover the square vent. This step creates an authentic look, while shutting out the cold air. Making sure the interior side of A2 is facing you (this is important because you want the three dowel holes to line up when you assemble the box) attach the other piece of vent backing in the same way.

9. Study the side view of the fireplace, as shown in figure 2, and lay out the front configuration of the fireplace. Once the cut lines are established, use a jigsaw, scroll saw, or coping saw to cut out the inverted U-shape.

Carve or sand away some wood from the front of the U-shaped piece to create the look of a rock and mud fireplace. The fireplace, once positioned over the hole on the side of the barn, will provide the opening through which birds will pass as they enter the roost box.

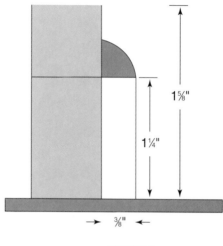

FIGURE 2

10. Center the fireplace on the bottom edge of one B piece, and draw a pencil line *inside* the inner edge of the fireplace. Use a jigsaw, saber saw, scroll saw, or coping saw to carefully saw out the entrance hole. Predrill, glue, and nail the fireplace in place.

11. Bevel the top edges of both B pieces to match the roof slant where the descending roof meets or converges with the front and back of the barn. Once the box is assembled, if there is a slight gap, seal it with vinyl caulk.

Assembling the box

12. Properly align the front, back, and sides, and slide the three dowels through the holes. Use 4d nails to assemble the pieces. Be sure all three roost perches line up before you nail the four major parts together.

13. Align the assembled box with the base. Once positioned, draw a line along the outside edge of the roost box onto the base. Remove the roost box. Cut out the square you have drawn.

14. In order to make the floor detachable from the base (for cleaning out the roost box) you need to add two interior closure jambs. Cut two lengths of ¾" plywood to fit *inside* the house, along the lower end of the front and back (figure 3). Glue and nail these pieces against the inside walls, flush with the bottom edge.

15. Drill two pilot holes into the bottom surface of each jamb, then drill four matching pilot holes in the floor. Use screws to attach the floor to the jambs. (When you mount the roost box on a treated wood pole, be sure to screw through the floor and into these jambs).

16. Lay the roost box on its left side with the entrance hole facing up. Measure up from the bottom 5¾" on the right side to locate the position for the shed roof anchor. Use glue and two 3d finishing nails to secure this triangle to the side, horizontal to the base (this anchor provides a gluing and nailing surface for the shed's roof bed).

Board and batten siding

17. To cut the siding boards, set your table saw or band saw to re-saw the 4/4- or 3/4 oak to a thickness of ¹⁄₁₆". Of the 20' of oak, 85 percent should be ⅜" wide and 15 percent should be ½" wide.

18. Cut the batten boards in the same manner as the siding. First re-saw them to a thickness of ¹⁄₁₆". Then re-set your saw fence and saw them ³⁄₁₆" wide.

19. Using glue and 20-gauge brads, begin siding the barn at the left corner of the box front, and continue to your right all the way around the box (skipping over the front door and above the door). Glue and nail the battens over the vertical cracks between each pair of vertical boards. Stagger your nails to avoid creating obvious nail lines.

20. Add the rain shed roof over the barn entrance door, using a piece of ⅛"-thick oak, with a beveled edge. Glue and nail it in place over the door. Cover this piece with split shingles (see step 21) before finishing the siding on the front of the barn.

Making and installing roof shingles

21. Follow steps 20 through 24 for the Appalachian Farm Smokehouse, on pages 27 to 28.

Adding the shed roof post

22. Chamfer an angle along the edge of G so it will fit the side of the box once the roof bed is positioned at its proper angle. Use a

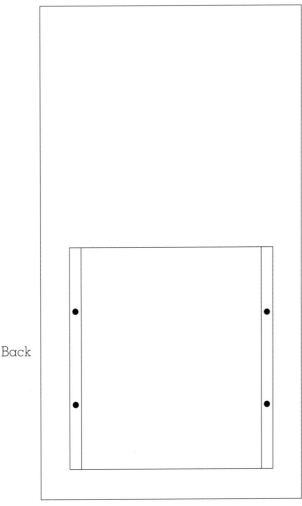

FIGURE 3

Back

Front

20-gauge brad to temporarily tack the roof bed in place.

23. Mark the position of the roof support posts on the base, below the trailing edge of the roof bed. Drill the two ⅜" holes, ⅛" deep. Glue and nail the posts in place.

24. Remove the brads in the roof bed and glue and nail the roof bed to the roof bed anchor. It should fit tightly against the side of the barn with equal overhang on both sides. Fasten the two braces to the shed roof and to the side of the barn.

25. Position the tops of the two posts under the roof bed and mark their location. Predrill

two holes through the roof bed directly above these marks, then glue and nail the posts to the roof bed.

26. Shingle the shed roof.

27. Paint the entire structure with flat black exterior latex paint, as described in step 25, page 28.

28. Cut the 18" long hardwood limb into 1"-thick pieces, each about 2" long. Use a ¾" wood chisel and mallet to split the oak into miniature firewood, removing the bark as you split. Use plenty of glue to fasten the wood to the base in stacks.

COLONIAL SALT BOX

DESIGNER: **CHRISTOPHER LAWING**

 Balsa clapboards and shingles transform a simple birdhouse into a handsome, miniature, New England classic.

CUT LIST

¼" plywood
> Front/back: 4⅜" x 12" (2)
> Sides: 4" x 8" (2)
> Floor: 4" x 4" (1)
> Roof: 5" x 4½" (1), and 5" x 4¾" (1)

³⁄₃₂" balsa
> Clapboards: 1" x 4" (approx. 33)
> Shingles: 1" x 5" (approx. 15)

Balsa trim
> ¼" x ⅛" x 30" (1)
> ⅛" x ⅛" x 30" (1)

MATERIALS AND SUPPLIES

½" brads
2 small brass hinges and screws
Carpenter's glue
Paintbrush
Acrylic finish

TOOLS

Circular saw or jigsaw
Drill with ⅜" and ¼" bits
Hammer
Screwdriver
Craft knife

INSTRUCTIONS

1. On the front and back pieces, measure down 4" from one end along the sides, and cut to the midpoint to form the gables.

2. Drill a 1½" entrance hole on the front, centered, 6¾" up from the bottom and 2³⁄₁₆" in from the side. Drill a ¼" mounting hole on the back piece, centered, 3" down from the peak.

3. Assemble the front, back, and sides.

4. Drill holes on the bottom to match the holes in the hinges you selected, then mount one side of each hinge to the bottom. Drill matching holes on the floor-end of the front and back pieces, and mount the other side of the hinges. (These can be removed when you want to clean the box.)

5. Angle the ends of the roof pieces and nail them in place.

6. Cut the ⅛" balsa trim to fit the outer sides of the front, and glue in place. Cut the ¼" trim so it is flush with the ⅛" trim on the front and flush with the sides along the back. Glue on the trim, cutting as necessary to assure a good fit.

7. Cut the clapboards to fit, and glue them evenly up the sides and front, overlapping them by ¼". Using the same technique, cut and glue the shingles to the roof. Use the ¼" balsa to trim the edges of the roof. Glue on a piece of trim where the shingles meet at the roof peak.

8. Apply at least two coats of a clear, acrylic finish and let dry.

A-Frame

DESIGNER: **ROBIN CLARK**

Birds with a discerning eye will swoon for this timeless design, perfect for hanging in a tree or on your back porch.

CUT LIST

1" cedar
- A—Side: 7" x 11¼" (1)
- B—Side: 7" x 10" (1)
- C—Front/back: 6⅞" x 8" x 8" (2)
- D—Floor: 4¼" x 5½" (1)

⅜" dowel, 2" long (1)

MATERIALS AND SUPPLIES

Wood glue
1¼" decking screws
Heavy-gauge copper wire, 36" long
Sandpaper
Fine-tipped permanent black marker
Ruler

TOOLS

Table saw
Jigsaw
Drill with ⅛", ⅜", and 1⅛" bits
Phillips screwdriver
Wood-burning tool (optional)

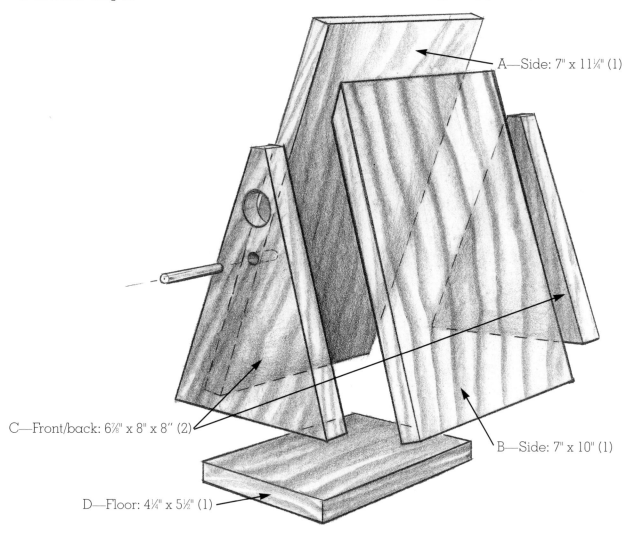

A—Side: 7" x 11¼" (1)

C—Front/back: 6⅞" x 8" x 8" (2)

B—Side: 7" x 10" (1)

D—Floor: 4¼" x 5½" (1)

INSTRUCTIONS

1. Cut off the tops of the triangles on both C pieces (this creates a gap below the roof line for ventilation).

2. On the C piece that will be the front of the birdhouse, center and drill a 1⅛" hole, 5½" from the bottom, to create the entrance hole. Drill a ⅜" hole, ¼" deep, 3⅞" from the bottom. Then, drill a ⅛" pilot hole, centered, 1⅛" from the bottom.

3. Drill a ⅛" pilot hole, centered, 1⅛" from the bottom on the other C piece.

4. Screw the front, back, and floor together .

5. Cut a 45-degree angle at one end of B. Then drill three evenly spaced ⅛" pilot holes, ⅝" from the angled edge.

6. Position the angled edge of B against one end of A so that the squared sides of both pieces rest on your work surface. On B, drill three ⅛" pilot holes down both sides, 1" in from the edge, and about 2½" apart. On A, drill two ⅛" pilot holes down both sides, 1" in from the edge—the first 2½" from the bottom, and the other 5¼" from the bottom.

7. Position A and B over the assembly of the front, back, and sides, and carefully attach A and B with screws.

8. Glue the dowel in the predrilled ⅛" hole below the entrance hole.

9. Thread the copper wire through the gap below the roof line and wrap the ends around each other to create a loop.

10. Sand all the edges.

11. Finishing: Using a ruler as a guide, mark horizontal lines with the black marker, evenly spaced in rows (or you can wood burn the lines). Add the vertical lines and shading to create the effect of shingles.

DOWN TO BRASS TACKS
I AND II
DESIGNER: **TERRY TAYLOR**

To create this appealing pair of nest boxes, designer Terry Taylor embellished ready-made birdhouses with a style of ornate wood carving called tramp art. *Popular in America from about 1875 to 1930, it was practiced by artists (not tramps!) who often whittled cigar boxes and fruit crates.*

MATERIALS AND SUPPLIES

Wooden birdhouse, any size and shape
Basswood sheets, ¼" thick*
Basswood sticks ¼" x ¼"*
Pencil
Acrylic craft paints in colors of your choice
Paintbrushes
½" brads
Carpenter's glue
Decorative upholstery tacks in brass or silver finish
Acrylic matte sealer
available in a variety of lengths and widths at craft-supply stores

TOOLS

Small jigsaw or other saw for making accurately cut shapes
Carving knife or pocketknife
Clamps
Hammer
Awl

INSTRUCTIONS

1. Determine which surfaces of your birdhouse you wish to embellish. The roof, front, and sides are good places to start. Lightly sketch out the general shape you want, such as a large rectangle on the roof, a series of rectangles along the sides, or interlocking triangles. A general rule of thumb for tramp-art carving is that each layer is smaller than the one it rests on. For instance, if you are using ¼" basswood, a 4" x 7" rectangle would have a second layer that measures 3½" by 6½". You simply reduce each layer proportionally to the thickness of the material.

2. Measure each of the shapes you have sketched and transfer these measurements to the sheet of ¼" basswood. Cut out the shapes with a suitable saw.

3. Use the rule of thumb described in step 1 to determine how large to make the succeeding layers—make as many layers as you wish. The finest examples of tramp art have many, many layers, which give the piece its complexity.

4. Use the carving knife or pocketknife to make v-cuts on the edges of each piece. First make a shallow, straight cut about ⅛" deep, and then angle the knife at either side to complete a v-cut by carving toward the straight cut. Your chip should "pop" right out. Use a scrap piece of wood to practice on until you are comfortable with the technique.

5. When you have finished chip carving all of your layers, set them aside, stacked in the order in which you plan to attach them to the house.

6. Paint the birdhouse with two coats of your chosen base color, allowing each coat to dry.

7. It is intriguing to use contrasting colors for the layers, but you can paint the house and the layers one color. For contrasting color layers, paint each piece that you have chip carved with two coats of acrylic enamel, allowing each coat to dry well. If you wish to further define the chip carving, take a sponge-type brush and paint a contrasting color on the top of the piece. If you use a light touch, the paint will not go into the chip carved area. Let dry.

8. Coat the back side of the bottom layer of a section with carpenter's glue. Position it, clamp, and allow to dry. When dry (takes about 30 minutes), use brads to secure the layer. Continue in this manner to secure all the layers.

9. Now you can add the upholstery tacks. Mark the spot you want to tack, make a starting hole with an awl, and then tap the tack into position with a hammer.

10. Apply a light coat of acrylic sealer and let dry.

Log Cabin Birdhouse

DESIGNER: **Darlene Polachic**

This cozy cabin, with its willow branch logs, is ready to provide a snug nesting place for nuthatches, wrens, chickadees, or downy woodpeckers.

Cut List

¼" plywood
> Roof: 6½" x 12" (2)
> Door: 2¼" x 4" (1)
> Windows: 2" x 2¼" (2)

¾" cedar
> Floor: 7" x 9½" (1)

Willow branches (or other straight branches) for the logs, ½" in diameter and the equivalent of 40'

Willow twigs (or other straight twigs) for the trim, ⅜" in diameter and the equivalent of 4'

SUPPLIES

Nontoxic wood sealer or varnish
Paintbrush
1" and ¾" brads
⅜" wood staples
Tar paper scraps
Diluted fabric dye bath (optional)

TOOLS

Whittling knife or sharp pocketknife
Handsaw or jigsaw
Coping saw or small backsaw
Hammer
Drill and 1/16" bit

INSTRUCTIONS

1. Coat the floor with nontoxic varnish or wood sealer and let dry.

2. You can strip or shave the bark off the log branches or leave them as you have found them. (If you strip off the bark, a further step would be to "antique" them by soaking them in a bath of diluted fabric dye.)

3. Cut two 12" logs from the ½" willow. Measure in ⅜" from one end and mark. Measure in 2⅜" from the other end and mark. Working inward from the marks, whittle a ½"-long and a ¼"-deep notch at each point (figure 1). These two logs will be the supports for the perch. Lay them, notched side up, 2½" apart lengthwise down the center of the floor. Tack the logs to the floor with 1" brads. If the wood splits, you may have to predrill holes.

4. Cut two ½" x 10" logs. Measure in ⅜" from both ends and carve ½" notches, ¼" deep, as before. Nail these foundation logs, notched side up, lengthwise, one along each edge of the floor.

FIGURE 1

5. To complete the foundation, cut two ½" x 8" logs. Measure in ⅜" from the ends—or whatever it takes to match the edge logs—and cut notches as before. Lay these, notched side up, into the notches of the four lengthwise logs, across the width of the house. Nail them in place at the joints with ¾" brads.

6. Using the same measurements and method, continue building the walls until nine lengthwise and eight widthwise logs are in place. Later, you will cut a 1¾" entrance hole through the fifth, sixth, and seventh logs at the perch end of the house, so use ¾" brads to fasten those logs to each other on both sides of that planned opening.

7. The ninth course of end logs will need to be cut shorter, with the notches closer together, to form the roof gables. Make them 7½" long, then measure in ¾" from each end and carve the ½" notches as before. Nail them in place, notched side up. Continue laying the sidewall logs as usual, fitting each into the whittled notches at the end walls of the house.

8. Cut the 10th course of end logs 6" long, the 11th course 5" long, and the 12th course 3" long. The 10th- and 11th-course logs are notched the same as the ninth; the 12th-course logs are notched directly in the center. Nail these courses in place.

9. Cut a 10"-long ridgepole and carve ¼" x ½" notches into it where it joins the two uppermost end logs. Place the ridgepole in the notches of the gable ends, notched side up, and nail in place.

10. Cut two 2"-long logs and nail them into the ridgepole notches.

11. With a saw, carefully trim the ends of the widthwise logs at an uniform angle.

12. On the perch end of the house, measure 3" up from the bottom and draw a 1¾" circle. Use a coping saw to cut through the fifth, sixth, and seventh courses of logs. (This circle can be rough as it will be covered by the plywood door.)

13. Cut a 1¼" hole in the upper half of the door piece and center it over the entrance hole. Nail the wood to the logs, then trim with ⅜" twigs. Cut another twig for the doorknob and nail in place. Then, cut three ⅜" twigs, 4¼" long, and nail them across the ends of the perch logs to make a little porch.

14. Nail the two windows in place and trim them with ⅜" twigs.

15. Butt the two roof pieces together at a right angle and fit the roof in place, allowing a 1" overhang front and back. Nail in place. If you desire, you can seal the ridge joint with tar or silicone, and cover the wood with tar paper or shingle scraps stapled in a few places.

16. Apply a coat of varnish or wood sealer. If you wish, you can tack on a wooden sign and wood burn the name of your special birdhouse. Mount the house from the bottom, using a bracket or post.

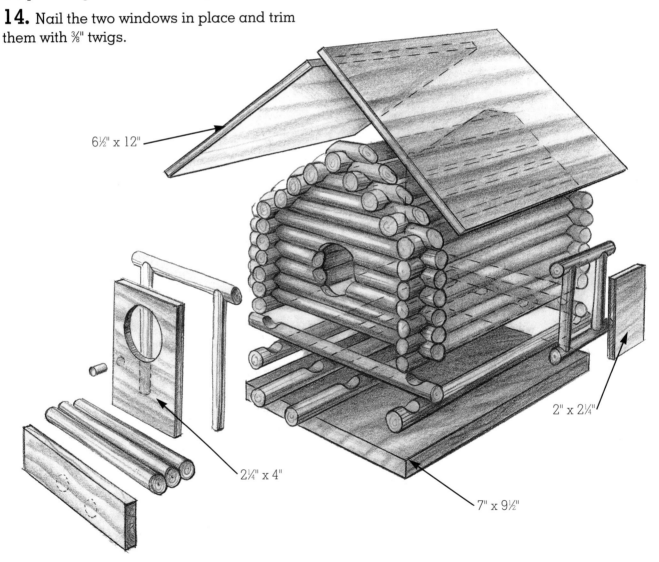

6½" x 12"

2¼" x 4"

2" x 2¼"

7" x 9½"

A variety of flowering plants that produce berries are a good addition to well-stocked bird feeders, and are very popular with many birds, such as the chickadee (top) and the warbler (bottom).

EGYPTIAN BIRDHOUSE CD CABINET

DESIGNER: **DIANE WEAVER**

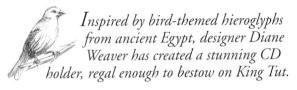

Inspired by bird-themed hieroglyphs from ancient Egypt, designer Diane Weaver has created a stunning CD holder, regal enough to bestow on King Tut.

CUT LIST

Floor dividers: 1" x 1" x 21" wood strips (2)
½" x ½" x 21" wood strips (2)
Shelves: 4½" x 5" x ¼" fiberboard (3)
Wooden disks: ⅛" plywood, 2½" in diameter (3)
Wooden ball, 2½" in diameter, halved (1)
Wooden dowel, ¼" x 2" (3)

MATERIALS AND SUPPLIES

Four-story birdhouse*
Wood glue
½" brads
Sandpaper
Wood filler
Paintbrushes
Black gesso
Box of white 2-ply facial tissue
Decoupage adhesive
Acrylic paint, mocha, black, and colors of
your choice
Acrylic sealer
Metallic gold leaf paint
Sponge
Hinges and screws
*available at craft-supply stores; this one
measures 7" x 7" x 25", and the measurements
for additional lumber are based on
these dimensions.

TOOLS

Saber saw
Drill and ⅛" bit
Hammer
Screwdriver

INSTRUCTIONS

Building the cabinet

1. Remove the roof and the base of the birdhouse. Cut through the three trim boards (figure 1) that separate the floors along the seams of the front panel. Remove the front panel. Remove the floor trim boards from the main body of the house, noting which board went where for the side boards, and discarding the boards from the back.

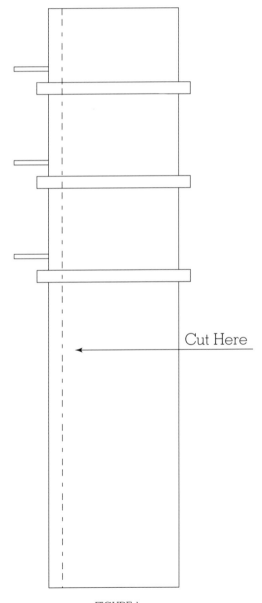

Cut Here

FIGURE 1

2. Glue in the fiberboard shelves and tack them at the back and sides where the floor trim will cover the tacks. Leave enough room between the shelves to accommodate the height of the CDs.

3. Glue and nail the ½" wood strips flush with the side edges of the house on the inside front against the shelves. Glue and nail the 1" x 1" strips on top of the ½" strips, making sure they lie flush with the outside of the box.

4. Reglue the trim boards to the sides of the house. They will now fit flush with the new front and the back.

5. Reattach the roof and base flush with the back of the cabinet.

6. Sand ⅛" off the top of the door so that it will open and close easily without binding the roof.

Decorating the cabinet

7. Glue the halved wooden ball and the three disks into the entrance holes in the front panel.

8. Sand, fill, and apply black gesso to all surfaces of the house, the halved wooden ball, the three wooden disks, and the three dowel perches.

9. Find Egyptian hieroglyphs you like in reference books in your local library. Copy them on good-quality lightweight paper so that they will fit each panel of the birdhouse. You may have to piece these patterns together from several separate hieroglyphs.

10. Using a flat 1" brush, apply a coat of decoupage adhesive to one section on the side of the house (not on the trim boards). Separate the two plies of a tissue and apply one layer over the wet surface, smoothing it down with the paintbrush. Apply a coat of decoupage adhesive over the top of the tissue, and in the same manner, add additional tissue and coats of decoupage adhesive until you have built up five layers, top-coating everything with the adhesive. The tissue will wrinkle—that is desirable—but pat down any large wrinkles and air bubbles.

11. While the surface is still wet, apply one of the paper copies of a hieroglyph, and cover it with decoupage adhesive. Continue applying the hieroglyphs and the adhesive, until you have covered all the side panels. Repeat step 9 on the front panel and then apply the hieroglyphs, cutting the paper to accommodate the entrance holes and the ball in the top hole.

12. Apply tissue and decoupage adhesive to the inside of the panel to cover the back of the disks (this will hide any gaps that may show around the disk).

13. Paint a mocha wash over all the panels on the outside of the box, keeping the wash light and transparent on top of the hieroglyphs. Let dry.

14. Paint in the designs with the colors of your choice. You may wish to consult your reference material to keep the colors authentic.

15. Glue on the perches.

16. Use a wet sponge to apply the gold acrylic paint to the base, floor trim boards, and roof. Apply the gold paint to one surface at a time and dab it off lightly to achieve the desired effect before the paint dries. If you don't like the effect, wipe the paint off and repeat the procedure.

17. Paint the shelves and the interior of the cabinet black. When dry, accent the outer edge of the shelves with gold acrylic paint.

18. Coat all the painted surfaces with acrylic sealer and let dry.

19. Paint the halved ball with metallic gold leaf paint; use this paint on other areas you wish to highlight. Do not seal the metallic gold paint as it will dull the finish.

20. Attach the hinges to the inside of the base, 1¼" from the outside edge of the door, and then to the inside base of the cabinet.

GILDED BIRDHOUSE FLOOR LAMP

DESIGNER: **DIANE WEAVER**

You can make this elegant floor lamp with gold leaf paper or take a shortcut and use wallpaper with grapes and vines. Either way, the finished piece is sure to attract rave reviews.

CUT LIST

1" basswood
    Bottom shelf: 1" x 9"
    Legs: 1" x 22"
    Chimney: 2" x 2"

MATERIALS AND SUPPLIES

Four-story birdhouse*
2" wooden balls (4)
3" spindle connector screws (4)
Wood glue
Paintbrushes, including #4 and #6 round,
    1" and 2" flat
Wood filler
Sandpaper
Black gesso
Package of composition-leaf in gold,
    5½" x 5½" sheets
Foil adhesive and sealer
Gold metallic paint pen

Method #1:
    Wallpaper with gold background
        and fruit motif
    Acrylic paints in colors that complement
        wallpaper colors
Method #2:
    White transfer paper
        Colored pencils in raw umber, raw
            sienna, burnt ocher, and black
    Acrylic paints: yellow ocher, charcoal
        gray, burnt umber, light khaki, wine,
        violet, dusty lavender, purple, periwinkle,
        white, leaf green, yellow, and olive green
Lamp kit, with a 28" assembly rod
Black lamp shade
*available at craft-supply stores; birdhouse
    shown here measures 7" x 7" x 25"

TOOLS

Handsaw or power saw
Drill with ⅛" and ¼" bits

INSTRUCTIONS
Adapting the birdhouse

1. Drill a hole in the center of the roof to accommodate the lamp rod. Cut a 90-degree angle in the chimney piece from the edge to the center, and drill a hole of the same size (figure 1).

2. To assemble the base, drill holes 1½" in from the corner of the 9" board, and corresponding holes in the bottoms of the four legs and the wooden balls. Screw the

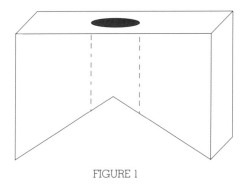

FIGURE 1

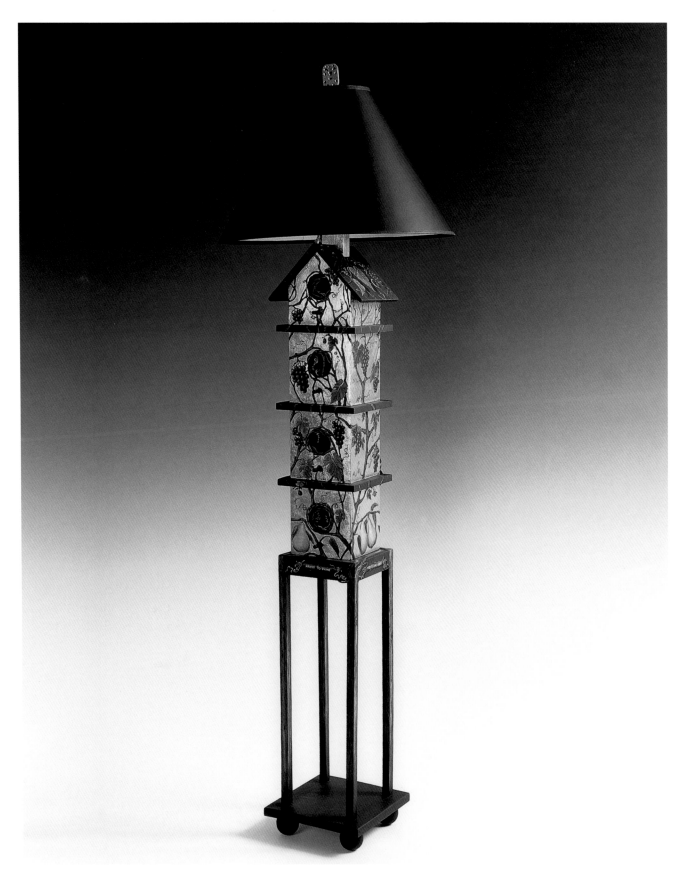

spindle attachments into the balls, then through the shelf, and into the legs (figure 2).

Painting the lamp

3. Fill, sand, and prime the base and the birdhouse with three coats of black gesso, sanding lightly between each coat. (You need a smooth surface under the gold leaf or the wallpaper.)

4. Paint the roof, floor dividers, and base with charcoal paint, and let dry.

Method #1

5. Measure and cut the strips of wallpaper that will wrap around each floor, but do not cover the floor dividers. You will need a small amount of wallpaper to wrap around the corners. Attach the wallpaper to the house.

6. Paint the trim between the floors and the roof with colors that complement the wallpaper colors.

7. Paint the foil adhesive on the chimney. Following the manufacturer's directions, apply the gold leaf. When you are finished, apply the sealer. *Skip to step 14.*

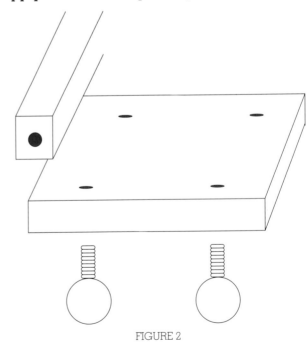

FIGURE 2

Method #2

8. Position and trace the pattern on the house using the transfer paper.

9. Paint the pears first with a mixture of one-third white and two-thirds yellow. While the paint is still wet, add little dabs of yellow ocher to the outside areas of the pears with a dry brush, then blend the colors using the same up and down motion. The dry brush technique is achieved by loading the brush tip with a small amount of paint. Test it on a piece of paper to make sure only a small, dry-looking amount of paint comes off with each brush stroke, allowing the background to show through intermittently.

Using the same technique, apply white to the top center of the pear's base circle, slightly blending the white into the yellow. When the paint is dry, use the burnt ocher, raw umber, and black pencil to add shading and form to the pears. Start with the black pencil, using light strokes at the bottom of the pear, following the contours with the direction of your strokes. Then add the raw umber, changing the direction of the strokes a little to come higher into the body of the pear and the bottom center. Last, use burnt ocher to shade the side contours of the pears.

10. Paint the vines with burnt umber to cover the transfer paper lines. Drag a dry brush with light khaki paint over the vines. Paint the individual grapes with the wine paint; leave an outline of black base coat showing through, but cover the transfer lines. Inside the wine color, apply a light coat of violet, leaving an edge of wine color showing, and blending the colors. While the grapes are still wet, paint on a coat of dusty lavender, purple, allowing the previous colors to show at the edges. When the paint has dried, add a large dot of periwinkle, and then add a small dot of white. The successive layers of

"move" to the upper left side of each grape, so that the white highlight ends up near, but not at the upper left of each grape. (Refer to the photo on page 110 for guidance.)

11. Paint the leaves using a dry brush technique. Start by painting the leaf's main vein with leaf green. Spread the bristles of your brush with your fingertips, place the brush tips against the vein, and pull the brush away toward the outside edge of the leaf. Soften this stroke by blotting it with your finger. Continue dragging the leaf in this manner, allowing the background paint to show through the dragged green. Highlight the leaf with the tip of your brush and a small amount of yellow paint. You can add

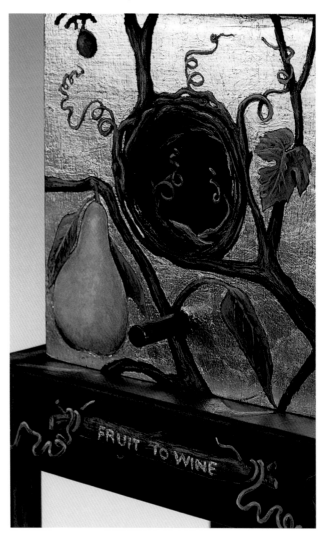

shadows with the olive green. Paint the vine curls with the leaf green, adding highlights and shadow as you did with the leaf. If any of the transfer paper lines still show, remove with a damp cotton swab when all the paint is very dry. Be sure to continue the vines and tendrils on the trim boards that divide each birdhouse level.

12. You can add more detail to the vines with colored pencils. Use raw sienna to show highlights on the left side of the wine, and ocher in the middle, leaving the burnt umber paint to fill in the right side. Use the black pencils for shadows.

13. Paint the foil adhesive on the black background that you wish to gold leaf and on the chimney. Following the manufacturer's directions, apply the gold leaf. When you are finished, apply the sealer.

14. Glue the chimney to the roof.

15. Attach the base to the birdhouse, sanding and touching up the paint as necessary. Trace the pattern and/or complete the base in the same manner as you did the house. Run the vine down all four sides of each leg, blending to black a few inches before the bottom of the base.

16. Around the top of the base, on the horizontal twig, write in gold metallic paint, one line per side:

> FRUIT TO WINE
>
> TREES AND VINES
>
> SOME GROW OLDER
>
> AND BETTER WITH TIME.

17. Wire the lamp according to the kit directions. Attach the lamp shade.

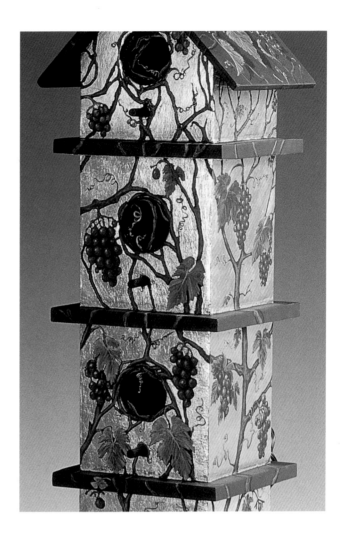

DISTRESSED BIRDHOUSE CLOCK

DESIGN: **DIANE WEAVER**

The finish and details on this charming clock can give new life and beauty to your favorite painted birdhouse that has been exposed to the weather over the years. Or, you can create this effect on a newly painted birdhouse.

Materials and Supplies

Two-story painted birdhouse, new or used
Dentil molding*
Colonial molding*
Roof peak topper*
Basswood board, ¾" x 10" x 4'
Basswood strips, ½" x ½" x 10" to 15"
Wooden disk, ¼" x 2"
4 wooden balls, 1½" in diameter
2 wooden dollhouse washboards
4 wooden dollhouse bowls, the largest size
    available
4 decking screws, 1½" long
½" brads
4 decorative hinges, ½" long
Hat rack peg, ⅜" x 2⅜"
Screw-on tin lid, such as the type used to top
    a cardboard tube, 2" to 3" in diameter
Clock parts (that match the thickness of the
    walls of your birdhouse)
Photocopy of an antique clock face or pocket
    watch, sized to fit inside the tin lid
Medium-grit sandpaper
Paintbrushes
Carpenter's glue
Acrylic paint of your choice
Sponge
Craft glue
Piece of thin cardboard
Black permanent marker
Acrylic sealer
*You will need anywhere from 5' to 9',
depending on the size of your birdhouse.
Measure your birdhouse before purchasing
the molding.*

Tools

Sanding block
Vise
Drill with ⅜" and ¼" bits
Handsaw or power saw
Metal miter box and saw
Jeweler's hacksaw or one with a very fine blade
Screwdriver
Tack hammer

Instructions

1. Sand off most of the paint on the birdhouse.

Making the base

2. Cut a square from the basswood board 3" larger than the bottom dimensions of the birdhouse. Draw a square 2¼" in from the edges of this square. Drill four tap holes through the wood, one at each corner of the square you have drawn. Glue the wooden balls into the wooden bowls. When dry, secure the balls in a vise, and drill tap holes through the center of the bowls and ½" into the balls. Attach the balls to the base with screws, making sure the screws are flush with the back of the base.

3. Cut two 1"-thick wood strips to fit inside the square you drew on the base. Glue them to the base, parallel to each other and flush with the pencil lines (figure 1). Measure and

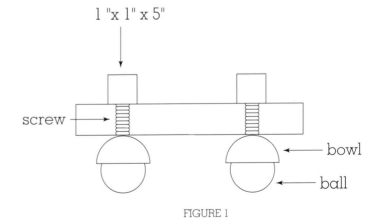

1 "x 1" x 5"

screw

bowl

ball

FIGURE 1

cut eight pieces of ¾" basswood using the miter box. The cut is a 90-degree angle, and the shortest side of the piece should measure the same as the length of the side of the birdhouse on which it will be attached. Glue and then tack four of the pieces around the bottom of the house, flush. Make sure the miters fit snugly. Glue and tack the other four pieces underneath the floor trim. Measure the outside dimensions of the trim and cut, glue, and tack the dentil molding to fit over the top of the basswood pieces, flush with the bottom of the house or with the underside of the floor trim board. Glue the base to the birdhouse.

4. Measure, cut, and glue the dentil molding under the eaves, front and back. When the glue has dried on this trim, measure, cut, and glue the colonial molding around the roof edge. Glue on the roof topper.

Decorating the clock

5. Using a dry brush technique (see the description in the Gilded Birdhouse Floor Lamp, step 9, page 109), apply a small amount of parchment colored paint or paint that matches your birdhouse to all the new moldings, the base outside the pencil lines, the legs, the hat rack peg, and both sides of the washboards. Let dry.

6. Here and there, add color highlights, using a color that complements the original birdhouse, and then wipe most of the paint off with a damp sponge. Add a little color to the washboards, too.

7. Drill a ⅜" hole ½" down from the lower entrance hole. Glue in the hat rack peg as a perch. Attach the washboards with hinges.

Mounting the clock

8. Drill a hole in the center of the wood disk to fit the clock shaft. Glue the disk into the top entrance hole. Use the hack saw to cut the top ⅛" off the tin lid, being careful not to

bend the sharp edges; you will need them sharp and straight so that you can drive them into the face of the house. Glue the copy of a clock face to a piece of thin cardboard. Punch a hole in the center for the clock shaft and cut the cardboard to fit inside the tin lid. Glue the cardboard clock to the front of the house, on top of the wood disk, aligning the holes. Use the black marker around the outer edge of the clock. Position the tin lid around the clock face, cover it with cardboard, and tap it into the wood.

9. Seal all the wood surfaces and the clock face with acrylic sealer.

10. Install the clock parts according to the manufacturer's directions.

GOURD BIRDHOUSE NECKLACES

DESIGNER: GINGER SUMMIT

These charming necklaces are truly irresistible. Make several to give as gifts to other bird lovers.

MATERIALS AND TOOLS

Ornamental gourd, cured

Bleach

Rubber gloves

Plastic dish pan

Plastic or metal kitchen
    scrubbing pad

Leather dyes in colors of
    your choice

Bird fetishes

Beads

Bamboo skewer

Craft glue

Wire brad

Waxed linen thread, 2 to 3 yards

TOOLS

Drill with ⅛" and ¹⁄₁₆" bits

Sharp knife

Wire cutters

INSTRUCTIONS

1. Clean the gourd as described in step 1 of the Floral Gourd Birdhouse on page 22.

2. Drill a ¼" entrance hole. Shake out the seeds through the hole.

3. Drill a ¹⁄₁₆" hole below the entrance hole. Drill a hole in each side of the gourd neck to string the necklace. Drill four holes in the bottom of the gourd to give the appearance of a real birdhouse with real drainage holes.

4. Color the gourd with leather dyes and let dry.

5. Cut the bamboo skewer 1" long. Put a dab of glue on one end and insert it into the hole below the entrance hole. Let dry.

6. Insert the wire brad through one of the bird fetishes and wrap the end around the "perch."

7. Cut the waxed linen into three strands of equal length, each 24" to 30" long, and slip them through the holes in the neck of the gourd. Position the gourd at the center of the strands, and hold it in place with tape.

8. Braid the three strands, braiding in a few bird fetishes as you work. When you are done braiding, slip on a few beads. Complete one end by knotting it; slip a bead onto the other end and knot it. Then slip the knotted end over the beaded end. Remove the tape.

GROWING GOURDS FOR BIRDHOUSES

Gourds make wonderful birdhouses for a variety of birds, such as Carolina, Bewick, and house wrens; chickadees; purple martins; violet-green and tree swallows; and bluebirds. Indeed gourds have been used for birdhouses for a long time; we know, for example, that Native Americans hung hollowed-out gourds from tree branches.

The type of gourd that makes the best birdhouses is the Lagenaria siceraria *or hardshell. Growing hardshell gourds is not difficult, but it does take patience; depending on their size, they can take three months to a year to dry or cure. The American Gourd Association (AGS) provides information on what type and size gourd you will need for the kind of bird you hope to attract. Gourd seeds of many varieties are available at most garden centers or through the AGS.*

Gourds require a long growing season. If you live in a northern region, start the seeds inside. Fill a pot with well-watered potting soil, put the seeds in the pot, cover with 1/2 inch of soil, then press down. Put the pot in a plastic bag and place in a warm place to allow the seeds to germinate. When a seedling appears within five weeks, the pot should be moved to a warm, sunny window and watered as needed. Transport the plant outside when the danger of frost has past.

Gourd vines grow very quickly and will grow up to four stories high if they have something to climb. When gourds begin to appear, you can shape them by tying ropes or cloth on them or by placing them in a container.

Once the vine has dried and turned brown in autumn and the gourds are mature (when they feel solid and firm to the touch), gourds can be harvested and cured. Most gourds, unless they are infected with disease, can be left outside to dry. They need to be turned once a week to insure even drying.

For information on growing and selecting gourds, contact the American Gourd Society, P.O. Box 274-P, Mt. Gilead, Ohio 43338. For more information on crafting with gourds, look for The Complete Book of Gourd Craft, *by Ginger Summit and Jim Widess (Lark Books, 1996).*

STENCILED KITCHEN LETTER BOX

DESIGNERS: **GEORGE HARRISON AND CATHY SMITH**

Minimize kitchen clutter with this beautiful cardinal-motif box. Mounted on the wall, it's the perfect home for the day's mail, and a handy place to hang your keys.

CUT LIST

1" maple

    Sides: 4¾" x 14" (2)

    Bottom: 4¾" x 8" (1)

    Front: 9¾" x 14" (1)

    Top: 7" x 11"

¼" plywood

    Back: 8½" x 13½" (1)

MATERIALS AND SUPPLIES

1" nails

2 small brass hinges with screws

Medium-grit and coarse-grit sandpaper

Paintbrushes, 1" flat bristle, and #0 round sable
    or synthetic sable

Damp cloth

2 sheets of smooth bristol board, 100 lb. weight,
    9" x 12"

Pencil

Transfer paper

Heavy piece of cardboard

Transparent cellophane tape

Household cellulose sponge, ½" to ¾" thick

Plastic tray or pallet

Acrylic craft paint in black, red-orange, cream,
    gold, burnt sienna, and sage green, leaf
    green, or light olive green

Brown acrylic antiquing gel

Spray acrylic gloss finish

Decorative hooks

Sturdy hook for hanging box on wall

TOOLS

Jigsaw

Table saw

Hammer

Drill with ⅛" bit

Scissors

Craft knife with #11 blade

INSTRUCTIONS

Building the box

1. Cut a ¼" dado on the top, bottom, and sides.

2. Insert the back into the side and bottom dados and nail in place.

3. Cut a ¼" x 5" slot in the center of the top piece and nail the top in place.

4. Cut the front into two pieces, each measuring 7" x 9¾". Drill a 2" hole in the center of the top section, 4" up from the bottom.

5. Drill pilot holes on the right-hand side of the lower section of the front to match the size of the screws that come with the hinges you have selected. Drill matching pilot holes on the bottom, right-hand side of the side piece. Attach the hinges.

6. Rout or cut a finger groove on the left-hand side of the hinged front section.

Painting the box

7. Use medium-grit sandpaper to remove splinters and provide the surface with "tooth."

8. Base coat all surfaces, inside and out, with red-orange paint. Apply at least two coats, letting each coat dry thoroughly.

9. After the last coat of red-orange is dry, paint the *outside* surfaces (but include the mail slot and the inner edge of the entrance hole) with one coat of black paint. Let dry in a warm place for at least 48 hours.

10. Using the coarse-grit sandpaper, sand off the black paint around the edges and on the body of the box to reveal some of the red base coat. Make the sanding patchy and uneven to achieve a worn look. Wipe the box with a damp cloth to remove the paint dust.

11. Transfer the stencil pattern (page 118) onto bristol board, using a pencil and transfer paper. Lay the pattern on a heavy piece of cardboard; be sure your craft-knife blade is sharp. Start the cut at the top of the line and cut towards yourself with firm strokes, being sure to cut all the way through the bristol board. Rotate the stencil so the line you are cutting is perpendicular to your body.

Do not tear any places that are not completely cut; use your knife to detach them.

12. Line up the center hole of the stencil with the hole in the box. Lightly tape in two places to hold the stencil securely while painting. Cut the sponge into five ½" strips—these are your brushes for the stencil. Wet the sponge strips thoroughly and squeeze out the all excess water. Note: While painting with the stencils, use one or two fingers to hold down the paper in the area that you are painting. This will help to give the stenciled image cleaner edges.

13. Cardinals: Pour a puddle of red-orange onto your pallet. Dip the end of a sponge strip into the paint and blot off the excess. Lightly dab the paint onto the cardinal portion of the stencil. Do not drag the sponge or press hard. Apply two coats of red paint, letting each coat dry. Create the black mask by dipping half of the end of a sponge in black paint (creating a triangle) and dabbing the bird once in the area behind the beak.

14. Dogwood blossoms, branches, and leaves: Lightly tape the stencils to hold them in place. Paint the flowers with cream paint, using a dab of burnt sienna on the tips of the petals. Blend this color with the cream for a pastel pink effect. Paint the leaves with green and the branches with burnt sienna. Carefully remove each stencil while the paint is still wet. Use the #0 brush to make green dots for the flower centers and then highlight the branches and the flower petals and centers with gold. Allow the paint to dry before moving on to another surface.

15. Floral border: Make heart-shaped leaves with green paint. Leave a little black paint showing for the center vein. The flowers are formed with three white brush strokes, with red dots in between the leaves.

16. When the paint is dry, use the flat brush to apply the antiquing gel to all outer surfaces. Let dry.

17. Spray the outer surfaces with two coats of acrylic finish. Let dry.

18. Screw the decorative hooks into the bottom of the box. Attach a sturdy hook to the back and mount the box on the wall.

COUNTRY COTTAGE BIRDHOUSE LAMP

DESIGNER: **MARGARET HAYES**

This charming lamp, with its playful birdhouse theme, features tiny birdhouses on the lamp base that are just the right size for the birds painted on the shade.

CUT LIST

1" pine

    Front/back: 7¼" x 12⅞" (2)

    Sides: 7¼" x 9" (2)

    Roof A: 6½" x 11¾" (1)

    Roof B: 7¼" x 11¾" (1)

    Front deck: 4" x 7¼" (1)

    Back platforms: ¾" x 1½" (2)

2" pine

    Chimney: 2" x 7" (1)

⅛" dowel, 8" long

SUPPLIES

1" screws

Craft sticks (12)

½" x ½" wooden beads (2)

Wooden shapes, ⅛" to 1" thick (2)

Miniature birdhouse on a dowel

Wood filler

Sandpaper

20 to 40 small stones

Carpenter's glue

Tracing paper

Pencil

Paintbrushes: ¾", ⅜", and ¼"

Liner brush

Acrylic primer

Acrylic paints in colors of your choice

Paint pens in white and black

Acrylic gloss varnish

15" blue lamp shade

Lamp kit with a 9" to 15" assembly rod with washer and nut

TOOLS

Bench saw

Drill with ⅛" and 3⁄16" bits

Screwdriver

INSTRUCTIONS

Building the birdhouse

1. Cut the wood as indicated and sand.

2. Cut 45-degree angles on the 7¼" sides of the front and back to form the peaks.

3. Drill four ⅛" pilot holes in the front and back pieces, ⅜" in from the side and 2" up from the bottom. Line up the edge of a side piece along the side of the front, and drill a 1" hole in the side of the side piece. Repeat with the other side piece.

4. Using the ⅛" holes drilled in the front as guides, drill 3⁄16" holes in order to countersink the #8 screws. Assemble the front, back, and sides with screws.

5. Use screws to fasten roof A and roof B onto the front and side, being sure that roof B overlaps roof A so that the roofline is even across the top.

6. Fill all the screw holes with wood filler, and sand when dry.

7. Drill a ½" hole through the chimney as shown in figure 1. Cut a 45-degree angle wedge 1" up from the bottom as shown. (Be sure to save the wedge to use in step 18 when wiring.) Drill a ½" hole through the center of the roof ridge. Center the chimney on the roof ridge, line up the two holes, and attach with carpenter's glue.

8. With the birdhouse on its side, apply a generous amount of carpenter's glue to one side of the chimney and gently press in the stones. Be sure the carpenter's glue completely covers the wood and is visible

FIGURE 1

FIGURE 2

between the stones; when dry, this will create the effect of mortar. When the carpenter's glue hardens, turn the house and repeat the process. Continue in this way until the chimney is covered with stones.

Painting the birdhouse and the lamp shade

9. Prime the birdhouse, the front deck, and the back platform, and let dry.

10. Paint the birdhouse ivory or a light color of your choice, and let dry.

11. Enlarge figure 2 (pages 122-123) on a copier to the desired size. Place the tracing paper on top of each pattern and trace over the lines with a sharp pencil. Turn the tracing paper over and color the entire back of the traced figure with pencil. Transfer the patterns onto the house by taping the tracing paper pattern, right side up, onto the appropriate side of the birdhouse, and tracing over all the lines. When you remove the paper, you should see the outlines of the pattern.

12. Paint the birdhouse, the front deck, and the back platform, using the photograph as a guide, or choose a different color scheme. Trim around all the windows, the door, and the painted hole with white paint pen. Use the black paint pen for the poles and for the string for the miniature birdhouses. Apply a light coat of varnish to the entire birdhouse and let dry.

13. Paint the wooden shapes to create miniature birdhouses in the desired colors; be sure to add a black dot for the "hole." When dry, glue the miniatures to the birdhouse.

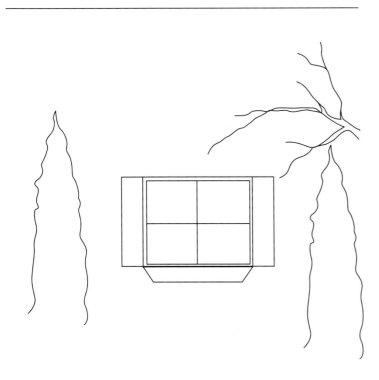

14. Paint birds and clouds on the shade.

Finishing and wiring the lamp

15. Drill a hole for the bird perch, centered ¼" down from the painted hole, and glue in a 2"-length of dowel. Drill a hole in the front deck and glue in the 4"-piece of dowel. Then glue on the miniature birdhouse.

16. Cut six craft sticks 2¼" long for fence posts and four sticks 3" long for side rails; use two uncut sticks for front rails. Attach them with carpenter's glue.

17. Glue on the front deck and the back platform pieces, making sure the platform pieces are completely under the house and flush with the sides and back.

18. Thread the lamp rod through the wedge you cut in step 7, and through the holes in the roof and the chimney (see figure 3). Then add the washer and the nut. To complete the wiring, follow the directions provided with your lamp kit.

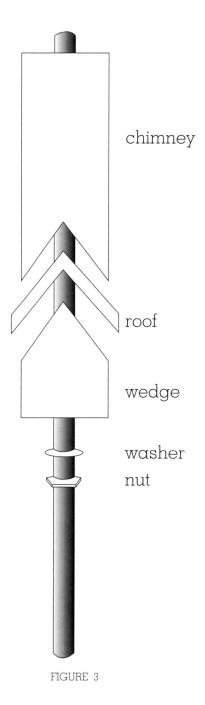

chimney

roof

wedge

washer

nut

FIGURE 3

NESTING BOX DIMENSIONS

Species	Floor of Cavity (inches)	Depth of Cavity (inches)	Entrance above Floor (inches)	Diameter of Entrance (inches)	Height above Ground or Water (W)(feet)	Preferred Habitat Codes
American Kestrel	8 x 8	12–15	9–12	3	10–30	1,4
Ash-Throated Flycatcher	6 x 6	8–10	6–8	*1½	8–20	1,6
Barn Owl	10 x 18	15–18	0–4	6	12–18	4
Barn Swallow	6 x 6	6	2	2	8–12	7,8
Bewick's Wren	4 x 4	6–8	4–6	1¼	5–10	2,7
Bluebird	4 x 4	8–12	6–10	*1½	3–6	1
Carolina Wren	4 x 4	6–8	4–6	*1½	5-10	2,7
Chickadee	4 x 4	9	7	1⅛	4–15	2
Downy Woodpecker	4 x 4	9	7	1¼	5–15	2
Flicker	7 x 7	16–18	14–16	2½	6–30	1,2
Great Crested Flycatcher	6 x 6	8–10	6–8	1¾	8–20	1,2
Golden-Fronted Woodpecker	6 x 6	12	9	2	10–20	2
Hairy Woodpecker	6 x 6	12–15	9–12	1⅝	12–20	2
House Wren	4 x 4	6–8	4–6	1–1¼	4–10	2,7
Nuthatch[1]	4 x 4	9	7	1⅜	5–15	2
Phoebe	6 x 6	6	2	2	8–12	7,8
Prothonotary Warbler	4 x 4	6	4	1⅜	4–12, 3W	3,5

Nesting Box Dimensions

Species	Floor of Cavity (inches)	Depth of Cavity (inches)	Entrance above Floor (inches)	Diameter of Entrance (inches)	Height above Ground or Water (W)(feet)	Preferred Habitat Codes
Purple Martin	6 x 6	6	1	2¼	10–20	1
Red-Headed Woodpecker	6 x 6	12	9	2	10–20	2
Robin	6 x 8	8	2	2	6–15	7
Saw-Whet Owl	6 x 6	10–12	8–10	2½	12–20	1
Screech Owl	8 x 8	12–15	9–12	3	10–30	2
Titmouse	4 x 4	9	7	1¼	5–15	2,7
Tree Swallow	5 x 5	6–8	4–6	*1½	4–15	1
Violet-Green Swallow	5 x 5	6–8	4–6	*1½	4–15	1
Wood Duck	12 x 12	22	17	4	10–20, 6W	3,5

*Precise measurements required; if diameter is over 1½", starlings may usurp cavity.
[1] Brown-headed and pygmy nuthatches (1⅛"), red-breasted nuthatch (1¼"), and white-breasted nuthatch (1⅜") will all use the same box. However, smaller opening sizes where appropriate may discourage use by house sparrows.
[2] One or more sides open.

Preferred habitat codes. The numbers in the last column refer to the habitat types listed here:
1. Open areas in the sun (not shaded particularly by trees), pastures, fields, or golf courses
2. Woodland clearings or the edge of woods
3. Above water, or if on land, with the entrance facing water
4. On the trunks of a large tree, or high in little-frequented parts of barns, silos, water towers, or church steeples
5. Moist forest bottomlands, flooded river valleys, or swamps
6. Semi-arid country, deserts, dry open woods and wood edge
7. Backyards, near buildings
8. Near water; under bridges, barns

Source: Reprinted from *Homes for Birds*, Conservation Bulletin 14, U.S. Department of the Interior.

CONTRIBUTING DESIGNERS

Robin Clark and his wife, **Helen**, own Robin's Wood Ltd, in Asheville, North Carolina, where they manufacture outdoor products for people and wildlife.

Harold (Hal) Hall is the president of the American Gourd Association. He lives in Kent, Ohio, and enjoys crafting with gourds.

George Harrison is a custom furnituremaker who lives in Weaverville, North Carolina.

Margaret (Peggy) Hayes creates custom painted furniture and cross-stitch designs. She credits much of her inspiration to her husband of 24 years, Charles. They live in Fletcher, North Carolina.

Christi Hensley lives on the side of Onion Mountain in Barnardsville, North Carolina. She enjoys working on a wide range of creative projects, from dollmaking, to birdhouse building, to rock painting. She enjoys giving her creations as gifts and selling them in specialty shops in Asheville.

Rolf Holmquist is an artist and printmaker who just moved into the cabin he built in Burnsville, North Carolina.

Susan Kinney is a papermaker, potter, jeweler, and interior designer who lives in Asheville, North Carolina.

George Knoll, of Leicester, North Carolina, handcrafts a variety of wood products, from fine jewelry boxes to rustic lamps and birdhouse made from fallen wood.

Christopher Lawing is a craftsman woodworker, who builds furniture, restores historical homes, and, on occasion, creates birdhouses. He lives with his wife and daughter in Asheville, North Carolina.

Shelley Lowell owns Pink Neck Gallery, an art gallery, in Asheville, North Carolina. A painter, sculptor, illustrator, and graphic designer, she received her BFA at Pratt Institute in New York, and now teaches a variety of art classes, including hand-painted furniture.

Darlene Polachic, who lives in Saskatoon, Saskatchewan, Canada, is a free-lance writer and avid crafter. She enjoys working in a number of genres, especially needlework.

Maggie Rotman is an artist who works in fiber and surface design. She lives in Asheville, North Carolina.

Pat Schieble keeps busy with trompe l'oeil and faux finish work for commercial and residential clients in the southeast. Creative and zany ideas spill over into painted furniture, and, on occasion, birdhouses. She lives in Mebane, North Carolina.

Sheila A. Sheppard is a multi-media studio artist who lives in Jonesborough, Tennessee. She strives to maintain the "soul instinct" that fires her creative spirit. She loves working with polymer clay because it is "a hybrid child of earthen clay and a rainbow." She sells her work throughout the Southeast.

M.C. (Cathy) Smith is an artist who works in a variety of media. She is currently following her destiny in western North Carolina, accompanied and encouraged in this pursuit by husband, son, and assorted feline, canine and reptilian family members.

Thomas Stender fashions one-of-a-kind and limited edition furniture in a lyrical, witty, and romantic style. He also designs furniture and home decor products for Modulus and t.a.g. in Chicago, Felissimo in New York, and other clients. He and his wife, artist Carrie Seid, are principals of Stender•Seid Designs, Inc., and reside in Chicago, Illinois.

Don Stevenson, who lives in Morganton, North Carolina, retired from a career as a field executive with the Boy Scouts of America. In 1995, Don and his wife, Judy, began to travel through western North Carolina and eastern Tennessee in search of interesting farm buildings and historic structures, which, because of their architecture, could be re-created as birdhouses and feeders without changing their basic appearance. He sells these miniature replicas through private commissions and galleries.

Ginger Summit, co-author of *The Complete Book of Gourd Crafts* (Lark Books, 1996) has been fascinated by gourds ever since she retired from teaching eight years ago. She feels passionate about gourds and derives great pleasure from working with them. She lives in Los Altos Hills, California, with her husband, Roger.

Terry Taylor is an artist whose work takes many forms, including the pique-assiette technique for making mosaics, and the style of chip carving associated with tramp art. He lives in Asheville, North Carolina.

Diane Weaver and her husband, Dick, operate Gourmet Gardens herb nursery in Weaverville, North Carolina. She is the author of *Painted Furniture* (Sterling/Lark, 1995).

INDEX